Super Trading Strategies

Tapping the Hidden Treasure in the Markets

from

Azeez Mustapha

ADVFN BOOKS

Contents

TRADERS' Magazine

The Single Most Important Secret Behind My Success

"So much to know, so much to earn
So much wisdom to seek and learn
If we raise our hands, we'll touch the sky
Our beds are low, our dreams are high…"
Niyi Osundare

I was born into a poor family of many children, and my parents struggled desperately to survive economically. I am a first-hand witness of extreme poverty, suffering, job loss and a high unemployment rate happening in the environment where I used to live. If you are reading this and you think you are currently suffering, you probably did not suffer as much as I did.

Throughout my teenage years, I engaged in hard and exhausting manual labour to support myself and help my parents. This is one reason why I was fortunate enough to get an education.

In spite of this, I was able to perform well at school because I developed an intense love for reading when I was eight years old. I liked to read anything I could lay my hands on. This has helped me gain lots of knowledge in many fields such as electronics, computers, history, literature, etc.

When I was a young adult, the future looked bleak indeed! In spite of my knowledge, I was thinking of taking a loan to get a used car for commercial driving. However, I decided to teach at private schools for a time, for paltry pay, which managed to keep me alive.

In 2007, my uncle called me and advised me to learn Forex trading, because it was very popular in my country at that time. I found someone to train me, but sadly, it was a poor training, and I suffered in the market for the next few years.

No matter what I did I was losing money, until I got to a point where I began to think of doing something else with my life. I went to a friend's house and I saw an old copy of TRADERS' magazine on his table. I begged him to lend me the magazine.

I went home to read it and I was enthralled by what Dr. Van. K. Tharp, who was interviewed in the magazine, said about successful traders. There I was! So there are successful traders! What are their secrets? What do they do differently and how might I benefit from their thoughts, trading styles and principles?

Since then, I have not missed a single copy of TRADERS' magazine. The more I read the magazines, the more enlightened I get by the realities of trading. Adapting to the realities is what has enabled me to become a better trader, transforming my life. I get constant inspiration and encouragement by reading the magazines and this has kept me going; whereas some people who started trading when I first did have abandoned their careers.

Although I am not yet a millionaire, I am no longer a poor man. I believe I am already on my way to financial freedom. I believe things can only get better. I am now able to cater for my basic expenses while I am still able to save money. Most importantly, I am living a debt-free life.

In the magazines, you will come across many professional traders revealing their secrets, insights, knowledge, trading methods and advice through articles and interviews. These have to do not only with Forex, but stocks, options, futures and other types of financial markets. I believe millions of traders have been touched positively by TRADERS' magazines. With TRADERS' you have everything to gain and nothing to lose.

So I can say confidently that I began to experience a turnaround from the day I began to read TRADERS' magazine. By reading TRADERS' magazine, you will be able to discover your true trading self and your calling as a profitable trader.

What got me started was not physical capital, but mental capital. I realized that having the right knowledge is very important to my success as a trader, and this is exactly what TRADERS' magazine has been offering for many years. The markets that consume others because of poor and irrational trading approaches are the same markets that lift some people out of poverty, launching them on their way to financial freedom.

The staff at TRADERS' media GmbH are committed to help you. Once you experience what the magazines offer, you will be hooked.

TRADERS' primary aim is to help millions of people be the best they can be in the world of trading. They are committed to working with this goal in mind. The magazines are available as print and electronic copies, and luckily, you can even get some copies free.

Please do yourself a favour by subscribing to TRADERS' magazine at www.traders-mag.com and www.traders-media.de.

A trial will convince you!

Introduction to
Super Trading Strategies

Hello Readers:

In the last few years I have written three books titled *Lessons from Expert Traders* (published by Harriman House, May 2013), *Learn from the Generals of the Markets* (published by ADVFN, May 2014) and *What Super Traders Don't Want You to Know* (also published by ADVFN, March 2015).

The books profile the best traders and investors in the world – dead and alive. We reveal their stories, trading/investing styles and approaches, plus other things they think and do differently to make them stand out in this extremely competitive, but lucrative industry. The books contain invaluable lessons and secrets that can be used by speculators to bolster their mindset and career in an uncertain world of trading.

However, certain readers leave negative reviews (which are normal and deeply appreciated). The biggest reason for most of the negative reviews is that readers who bought the books hoped to find concrete and easy-to-use trading strategies, which are not in the books. Although the books contain tips and tricks that can be used to improve your trading, I think readers also need specific trading methods they can use to tackle the markets.

Some of the best trading strategies and methods on this planet can be found in TRADERS' magazine. I have been writing strategies for them for six years. In the past, I tended to ignore requests for strategies, but I have our readers' best interests in heart, so I decided to find a way to write a book about strategies.

I approached TRADERS' and requested their permission to reproduce some of the strategies I had written for past issues of

TRADERS' magazine. This book is now available only because TRADERS' was kind enough to allow us to reproduce some of the strategies. If you use the strategies you are expected to make average gains that are bigger than average losses over time.

This book contains eleven selected strategies for winning the battles on Forex markets. Some of them are also great for the stock and futures markets. You can even try some of them on simulation accounts for a few months, just to see how useful they are. I have had trainees and clients who have applied some of these trading strategies and made decent profits with them. I have personally seen students, trainees, clients and other traders who have been making decent money from the strategies in this book. You too can make decent gains by using the strategies as they were supposed to be used.

There are short-term, swing and positions trading strategies in the book. Some are good for part-time traders and some for full-time traders. Simply study the book and choose a strategy that fits you. I would be happy to hear your testimonies as you use one of these strategies to tackle the markets victoriously.

All the strategies in this book are property of TRADERS' Media GmbH (all rights reserved).

A Multiple EMAs Strategy

One Way by Which a
Trader Makes Money

Some think that following the line of least resistance comes with less accuracy which may make us experience some roll-downs. The reality is that a major trend tends to experience equilibrium phases and at the same time experience frequent corrections that allow smart speculators to enter the market at better prices – in the direction of the major trend. The multiple moving average strategy mentioned here shows one way of entering the markets at better prices, while making logical attempt to follow the dominant biases, especially during those transient retracements.

A Clearly Defined Trend

The FX markets remain the best trending markets in existence. When a particular currency pair or cross is trending strongly in one direction, it is easily identified on a daily chart or 4-hour chart when the EMAs (exponential moving averages) with different periods settings are sloping in the same direction. It is not prudent to trade against such a significant trend. Rather, it is prudent to look forward to joining the trend when the price temporarily gets corrected lower (or when it rallies temporarily in a clean downtrend). On MetaTrader, there are line charts, bar charts and candlestick charts. We prefer candlestick charts for this trading system.

It should be noted that experienced speculators feel their strategies are so powerful that they can enjoy prolonged pips accumulation. This feeling is justified when gains are realized from riding a long-term trend. What has become a secret of the institutional trader can also be used successfully by the retail trader. In the life span of every bias, there will be a period when there is a counter-trend move which may cause the bias to lose momentum or pause temporarily prior to continuation. Anything can lead to a counter-trend movement. Fundamental analysts will always find reasons for that. A counter-trend movement may come because speculators are no longer interested in a particular direction and are therefore pulling out their stakes. Yes, not all those who follow the same market direction will make money because of different entry prices, wide or tight stop-loss levels, wide or tight take profit levels and different trading expiration dates. In order to remain logical in our action, we must ponder these facts.

Examples

In the charts, these are the colours that are used for the EMAs:

- EMA(8) = blue
- EMA(21) = green
- EMA(40) = black
- and EMA = red

In order to see this system in action, let us look at Figure 1. We can see the USD/JPY in a very strong uptrend (4-hour chart). In 2014, this currency pair assumed one of its strongest bullish runs in recent times. The bullish movement started in July 2014 and ran till the end of that year. We want to go long in this kind of market. Nevertheless, it should be remembered that our risk is high and reward is low if we go long when price is above EMA(8). In Figure 1 you can see that the price tended to trade lower once it went above the EMA. The areas where these happened have been circled. We do not want to trade when price is above EMA(8).

F1) High Risk Entry Points

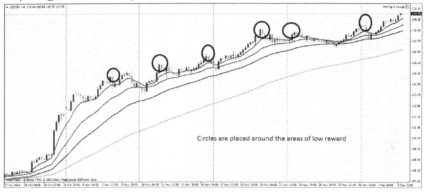

We want to go long in this kind of market.

In Figure 2, the same USD/JPY 4-hour chart is shown. Normally, we want to go long in this kind of market. Nevertheless, it should be remembered that our reward is high and risk is low only if we go long when the price dips into EMA(21) or EMA(40). This fact is also depicted in Figure 2, where you can see that the price tended to trade upwards once it tested EMA(21) or EMA(40). The areas where these happened have been circled. Here, we want to trade only when a bullish candle forms, following the test of EMA(21) or EMA(40) (on the condition that the price does not go far below each of the two aforementioned EMAs). This logic is reversed for a strong bear market.

F2) High Reward Entry Points

Circles are placed around the areas of high reward

Our reward is high and risk is low only if we go long when price dips into EMA(21) or EMA(40).

We need to know when we can ignore a market as well, for only a strongly trending market should be monitored for a possible entry signal. Do not trade a market that is moving sideways, which would be vivid when the EMAs are moving sideways. Do not trade a market in which two or three of the four EMAs are not sloping in the same direction with the rest. Do not trade a market in which the price has gone far above or below EMA(40), going towards EMA(100). Do not trade a market in which the price is testing or has just breached EMA(100), for that could be the beginning of a new long-term bias.

Figure 3 shows a market in which EMA(100) has been breached to the upside (AUD/USD daily chart). This can endanger the interests of the sellers, and we had better stay away from this kind of market. When EMA(100) has been breached to the upside or the downside, it could portend the end of the recent bias, plus it would take time for the four EMAs to align together in support of a new bias. The only market we want to trade is a market in which all the four EMAs are going in the same direction.

F3) An Example of When to Ignore a Market

This is a market in which EMA 100 has been breached to the upside (AUD/USD daily chart).

Trading Examples

It is essential to always set your stops and targets. This is a very crucial part of the system. When using this system to trade currency pairs and crosses, a stop of 100 pips (and a target of 200 pips) is recommended for each trade. But when using it to trade Gold and Silver, a stop of 200 pips (and a target of 400 pips) is recommended. This is because Gold and Silver tend to move faster in terms of pip gains and losses, when compared to currency trading instruments. In the charts, the red vertical line on the left shows where a trade was opened and the red vertical line on the right shows where a trade was exited. Spreads are not considered in these examples.

Example 1

In the EUR/CAD 4-hour chart (Figure 4), we can see that on 3 September 2014 the bearish trend was clearly visible in the market. All the four EMAs also supported the bearish bias. In the context of this downtrend, price had rallied into the EMA(40) before further rally was rejected as a bearish candle formed. A short trade was immediately initiated and it hit the target on the following day.

Respect the dominant bias in the market, irrespective of what the fundamentals may be saying.

F4) Multiple MAs – EUR/CAD Sell

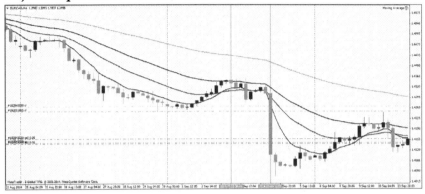

On 3 September 2014, the bearish trend was clearly visible in the market. All the four EMAs also supported the bearish bias.

Instrument: EUR/CAD
Order: Sell
Entry date: 3 September 2014
Entry price: 1.4300
Stop-loss: 1.4400
Trailing stop: 1.4200
Take profit: 1.4100
Exit date: 4 September 2014
Profit/loss: 200 pips

Example 2

In November 2014 the USD/CHF (Figure 5) had long been very strong, owing to continuous stamina in the dollar. You can see that the USD/CHF was trending strongly in the daily chart. Now, the trick was to join the uptrend and make money from it. But we would like to do that when things were temporarily on sale in the context of an uptrend.

That was exactly what we did and the trade was profitable. The market even moved far beyond our target – a movement of more than 600 pips. Nevertheless, we were happy with what the market gave us. In this same Figure, you can see a circle placed around where another profitable long trade would have been opened.

F5) Multiple MAs – USD/CHF Buy

You can see that the USD/CHF was trending strongly in the Daily chart. A circle has been placed around where another profitable long trade would have been opened.

Instrument: USD/CHF
Order: Buy
Entry date: 18 August 2014
Entry price: 0.9040
Stop loss: 0.8940
Trailing stop: 0.9140
Take profit: 0.9240
Exit date: 4 September 2014
Profit/loss: 200 pips

Conclusion

Super traders expect a losing streak that can stretch as far as several or many trades in a row. They accept this normalcy and that is why they are successful. When this trading system is followed as recommended, we would come out victorious as the least amount of mistakes is made. We do not make a mistake when we lose; we make a mistake only when we violate our rules. We ought to embrace this fact, and learn from our mistakes by not repeating them.

Strategy Snapshot	
Strategy Name:	A Multiple EMAs Strategy
Strategy Type:	Trend-following
Time Horizon:	4-hour charts for full-time traders, and daily charts for part-time traders
Indicators:	EMAs 8, 21, 40 and 100
Setup:	Seek long trades only when EMAs are sloping upwards; seek short trades only when EMAs are sloping downwards
Long Entry:	When a bullish candle has formed after the price has pulled back into EMA(21) or (40)
Short Entry:	When a bearish candle has formed after the price has rallied into EMA(21) or (40)
Stop-Loss:	100 pips when price has bounced off the EMA(21) or the EMA(40). 200 pip-stop is recommended for Gold and Silver
Position Size:	0.01 lots for each $2,000
Take Profit:	200 pips (or 400 pips for Gold and Silver)
Breakeven Stop:	Can be set after a gain of about 80-100 pips
Trailing stop:	Can be set after about 50% of the target has been achieved
Exit:	Any open position can be smoothed manually after 30 days

Effective Divergences Trading

Correctly Anticipating
Reversals Before They Happen

Have you ever heard of divergences in the market? What are they? What do they portend and how can serious traders take advantage of trading opportunities proffered by these chart pattern phenomena? This chapter attempts to answer these questions and it comes up with a strategy that can be used to trade divergences in an effective manner.

Divergences – the Power of Simplicity

Divergences remain one of the most popular trading approaches in the trading sector. They have been employed in harnessing decent gains from market action as compared to indicator readings. Divergence happens when a trading instrument moves to one side and an analytical tool slopes to another side. This phenomenon happens when an analytical tool reacts faster to changes in market data, than the price itself, and especially when the trend in the market is less significant. It basically means that the indicator and the price move in the opposite direction.

Without events, there cannot be history. Traders are blessed with historical data that is easily accessible to them in various formats and in charts. When we look at recent history and analyse its relationship with a good indicator like the On Balance Volume (OBV) we can detect some nuances. There are two types of divergence. One is bullish (positive) divergence and the other is bearish (or negative) divergence.

A bullish (positive) divergence occurs when the indicator goes upwards while the price is yet to form new highs, because both of them have to form new highs at almost the same time (under normal conditions). A bullish or positive divergence shows that the price could soon go upwards, just in conjunction with what the indicator is doing.

A bearish (or negative) divergence occurs when the indicator goes downwards while the price is yet to form new lows, because both of them have to form new lows at almost the same time (under normal conditions). A bearish or negative divergence shows that the price could soon go downwards, just in conjunction with what the indicator is doing.

Using the Trading System

It is important that you fully understand how your preferred system works. This is more important than having a wonderful system that you do not understand. On 4-hour charts or daily charts, we use EMA(8), EMA(21), EMA(40) and EMA(100). When these four powerful tools are sloping in the same direction, it means the trend is very strong. That is the type of the market we want to trade with the system.

We use different colours for the EMAs so that we can easily see what each EMA is doing, based on the dominant bias in the market, whether bullish or bearish. With EMA(8), we do not want to go long when the price pulls back into it (or go short when the price bounces towards it), because the risk-to-reward outcome may not be satisfactory. We do not go long when the price is above EMA(8), or go short when the price is below EMA(8), for the risk of being stopped out unnecessarily is high. But it is far better to go long when the price pulls back into EMA(21) or EMA(40) (or go short when the price bounces upwards into it).

Our stop-loss – our life insurance in the markets – should always be kept in place. This saves us from significant "crashes and rallies" that may have adverse effects on our positions. We keep out irrational emotions and subjectivity when trading. It is OK when we enter the market based on our criteria, and it is OK when we manage our trades according to our predefined parameters. You must try your best not to do anything that is contrary to your trading plan.

Approaching the Market with Positive and Negative Divergences Method

We use On Balance Volume (OBV) for this strategy because it has proven to be a good analytical tool for this speculation method. (See the definition at the end of the chapter for a further explanation for the indicator.) The OBV tends to move in unison with the price, and when there is a rise in the price momentum, we want to see that the OBV is signalling this rise as well. Otherwise, a pullback can occur. When the OBV rises, the bulls' positions gain strength and when it declines, the bears become stronger. Positive and negative divergences can be sought on hourly charts, 4-hour charts and daily charts, depending on where the divergences are seen. Divergences occur rarely, but when they occur, they may signal possible market reversals. However, a divergence between an indicator and a price does not always proffer assurance that the trend must change.

In Figure 1, we can see an example of bullish divergence in the AUD/NZD hourly chart. This is indicated by the oval shape in the chart. At this point, the OBV started sloping upwards gradually when the price still consolidated. Later there was a serious bullish breakout which posed a threat to the recent bearish outlook in that market.

F1) Positive Divergence in the AUD/NZD Hourly Chart

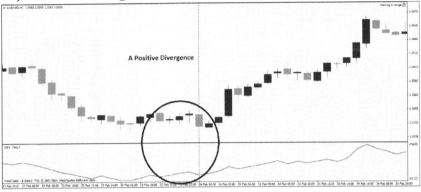

An example of a bullish divergence in the AUD/NZD hourly chart is indicated by the oval shape in the chart.

In Figure 2, we can see an example of bearish divergence in the Silver 4-hour chart. Silver was trying to make higher highs because the bulls were making desperate at tempts to push the price upwards, soldiering on, while the OBV was generally sloping downwards. It is not possible for a market to continue to go upwards while the indicator is going the opposite way – a reversal is bound to happen. There is no way a live poisonous snake and a live rat would live peacefully together in the same hole. The price plummeted afterwards.

F2) Negative Divergence in Silver 4-Hour Chart

Here too, we can see an example of bearish divergence in Silver 4-hour chart.

As in the examples above and below, divergence signals may sometimes happen quickly. Sometimes, they may drag on for a while, making them conspicuous in the markets.

Also take note of the position sizing and risk control recommendations that come with this strategy. Occasional negativity can be experienced, for this is not a Golden Goose method, but one can generate average winners that will constantly be larger than average losers. We do not need to be overconfident to the extent of risking more than what is recommended per trade, for multiple studies have demonstrated that human beings are prone to overestimate their abilities. The past losses gave us unique opportunities to learn good lessons and enhance our skills. While we cannot control the fundamental events that impact our speculation activities, we do have a choice. We can continue to brood over the mess or we can control our losses and profits.

More Examples of Positive and Negative Divergences

Divergences are subtle technical actions. You need to pinpoint and practice with them in order to familiarise yourself with the concept whenever it presents itself in the chart. In the examples, the red vertical line on the left shows where a trade was entered, while the red vertical line on the right shows where a trade was exited.

Trade 1

We take the first trading example from the EUR/CAD daily chart. There was a fierce tug of war between the bulls and the bears in the month of February 2015. This caused a kind of sideways movement in the market. However, it was noted that the OBV started going downwards while the market was still moving sideways. This signalled a bearish divergence and we went short on 23 February 2015. The trade was a success. Take a look at Figure 3.

F3) A Negative Divergence Leads to a Bearish Signal

The EUR/CAD daily chart.

Instrument: EUR/CAD
Time frame: 4-hour chart
Order: Sell
Entry date: 23 February 2015
Entry price: 1.4250
Stop loss: 1.4400
Trailing stop: 1.3935
Take profit: 1.3800
Exit date: 4 March 2015
Profit/loss: 450 pips

Trade 2

When we looked at a GBP/USD hourly chart in Figure 4, we saw that the market was generally in an equilibrium phase. On 10 February 2015, the price was moving indecisively when the OBV began to slope gradually upward. The thing continued into the following day (11 February), and early on 12 February, it was clear that price action was being marred by the bears' machinations, while the OBV kept on sloping generally upwards. In this kind of scenario, we should pay more attention to what the OBV is doing, not bothering ourselves with the bears' machinations. We should first chase away the fox before we scold the chicken. Therefore, the fact that the OBV was still sloping upwards meant that buying pressure was building up gradually. We opened a long trade and our target was attained on the same day.

F4) A Positive Divergence Brings a Bullish Signal

GBP/USD hourly chart showing the market generally in an equilibrium phase.

Instrument: GBP/USD
Time frame: Hourly chart
Order: Buy
Entry date: 12 February 2015
Entry price: 1.5220
Stop loss: 1.5070
Trailing stop: 1.5325
Take profit: 1.5370
Exit date: 12 February 2015
Profit/loss: 150 pips

Conclusion

Sometimes we expect trading to be satisfactory and pain-free, but this does not happen in reality. For trading professionals, it is a place for constant development through both good and bad trades. Once again I implore you seriously to stick to the risk and money management rules of this unique strategy, not allowing greediness to mar your objectives. Greediness breeds discontent, leaving traders unsatisfied with small and consistent profits and robbing them of the kind of happiness enjoyed by sane risk managers. When you find it irresistible to beg too big on each trade, then you are a problem gambler, not a trader. According to one source, problem gambling has plunged addicts into debt or even bankruptcy and has cost many of them jobs, marriages, and friendships. Therefore, if you are aware of the dangers of betting too big and gambling, you would find valid reasons for avoiding them as you journey towards trading mastery. Being a good trader is priceless!

Definition

The On Balance Volume (OBV) is a momentum indicator that uses volume flow to predict changes in stock price. OBV is a metric developed by Joseph Granville in the 1960s. He believed that, when volume increases sharply without a significant change in the price, the price will eventually jump upward, and vice versa.

The theory behind OBV is based on the distinction between smart money – namely, institutional investors – and less sophisticated retail investors. As mutual funds and pension funds begin to buy into an issue that retail investors are selling, volume may increase even as the price remains relatively level. Eventually, volume drives the price upward. At that point, larger investors begin to sell, and smaller investors begin buying.

Strategy Snapshot	
Strategy Name:	Positive/negative Divergence Trader
Strategy Type:	Swing Trading
Suitability:	Part-time trading
Time Horizons:	Hourly charts, 4-hour charts, or daily charts
Indicator:	On Balance Volume (OBV), default parameters
Setups:	Sell when the OBV slopes downwards while the price is yet to follow suit (bearish divergence) and buy when the OBV slopes upwards while the price is yet to follow suit (bullish divergence)
Position Sizing:	0.01 lots for each $2,000 or 0.1 lots for each 20,000 cents in a cent account
Stop-Losses:	50 pips for hourly charts, 100 pips for 4-hour charts and 150 pips for daily charts
Targets:	Choose a take profit that is three times greater than the stop loss
Risk to Reward Ratio:	1:3
Breakeven:	Move your stop to breakeven after the initial risk has been covered
Trailing Stop:	You may use a 50-pip trailing stop after about 70% of your target has been covered

Trading Around Great Psychological Levels

How to Go Along With Dominant Forces in the Markets

There are important price levels in the markets – the so called psychological levels. These levels are difficult to breach, but once they are breached, there is a great likelihood that the dominant market force that aids the breach may continue for a considerable period, and the continuation may take several weeks or months. This chapter discusses one way of trading with this interesting idea.

The Idea Behind the Strategy

These psychological levels are important because they are difficult to breach to the upside or to the downside; and once they have been breached, the market forces that enable the breach could continue for a long time. When a significant support level is breached to the downside, it becomes a significant resistance level which is no longer easy to breach to the upside again, which means that the price may continue going south.

This is also true of when a significant resistance level is breached to the upside; it becomes a significant support level, aiding the bulls. The auspicious bullish forces may thus enable the determined bulls to contend with the cantankerous bears for supremacy. Wise traders would then want to join the bullish effort after a correction may have panned out. When some unwise traders notice bearish corrections, they might rush to cover their positions, thinking that bearish moves have started. When there are bearish corrections, the bears think that they have been smart by going against the trend. People do not fail in the markets because they know nothing, they fail in the markets because they do not know enough. At times, it is better to follow the trend during corrections, for one may be stopped out unnecessarily when one follows a trend when it is currently strong. When a great level is approached, there may be a serious struggle between the bulls and the bears, leading to great volatility around the level, which may result in a failure to breach the level. Should the level then get breached and the price closes above or below it, it may signal a new lease of sustained trending movement.

As mentioned earlier, there may sometimes be a lot of volatility and equilibrium around an important market level, prior to the inevitable breach of the level or the failure of the price to breach the level. Following a trend is a consolidating phase, which shows that the market starts consolidating after a trending move.

The consolidation is brought about by the bears' and the bulls' attitudes, which have become cold, as cold as the dog's nose. The market also trends seriously after the consolidation. When a price has been in the consolidating phase for a considerable amount of time, it means that there will soon be a serious movement to the upside or to the downside. When a breakout, say to the downside, does occur, we would not want to leave our long orders at the mercy of the bears. That would be like entrusting your chicken to the care of the fox.

A typical significant level would have four or three zeros, though a level with four zeros is more significant than a level with three zeros. An important psychological level on the USD/JPY is 110.00 (three zeros), but the level at 100.00 (four zeros) is even more important. When the USD/JPY breaks the level 100.00 to the upside or downside, the bearish or the bullish force that achieves that feat would be strong enough to continue, bringing good profits for those who follow the direction. On the EUR/USD, the price level at 1.2000 or 1.1000 (three zeros each) is significant, but the price level at 1.0000 (four zeros) is more significant, i.e. when the EUR reached parity with the USD. These are examples of large round numbers in the markets. When the EUR reaches parity with the USD or the level 1.0000 gets broken to the downside, the bearish force that made it happen would be important enough to enable a continued bearish movement.

Trading with the Idea

We would need to draw a thick horizontal line in order to find it easy to see when an important round number (psychological resistance or support level) is challenged and/or breached to the upside/downside. If we want to apply a thick horizontal line to a chart in MetaTrader 4, we would go to "Insert" (beside "View") and then click on it. We would then click on "Horizontal Line." Then the cursor can be moved up or down on the chart. Once you click on the chart, the Horizontal Line appears; which is shown in the default colour red. You can right-click on the chart and select "Objects List," from where you can edit the Horizontal Line to make it thicker and/or change the colour. You can also delete it here, if you wish. Apart from this manual application, there are pieces of software that can also plot horizontal lines on the chart automatically, but we are only interested in horizontal lines that help us see large round numbers easily.

Let's check the Silver daily chart in Figure 1. You can see a thick horizontal line at 20.00, which is an important level. Whenever this great level gets broken downwards, the bearish pressure that pushes the market across the line will be strong enough to continue pushing the price downwards. The same thing is true of when bullish pressure pushes the price above the horizontal line. In the Silver chart, other horizontal lines can be drawn at 30.00 and 10.00. When you switch to the Silver weekly chart and apply the horizontal lines at 30.00, 20.00 and 10.00, and move your chart forwards, you can see how useful this idea is.

F1) Silver Daily Chart: Horizontal Line at 20.00

There is a thick horizontal line at 20.00, which is an important level.

Another instance is seen in the AUD/USD daily chart, in Figure 2. An oval shape is put around the area where the price crossed the thick horizontal line at 1.0000 to the downside. The market tumbles after the horizontal line is crossed to the downside and the price closes below it. In the future, when the price is able to reach that significant level of 1.0000 and crosses it to the upside, it is more likely that the bullish force that enables that to happen would be strong enough to continue aiding further journey to the north. Sometimes, the horizontal line acts as a formidable support in a bull market and as a formidable resistance in a bear market. While a psychological level like 1.0000 is very important, there are also important levels at 0.9000, 0.8000, etc.

F2) AUD/USD Daily Chart: Horizontal Line at 1.0000

The AUD/USD daily chart. An oval shape is put around the area where the price crossed the thick horizontal line at 1.0000 to the downside.

In addition to the horizontal line, the EMA 10 also helps us to easily determine the direction of the force in the market. Further details about the trading idea are revealed in the Strategy Snapshot at the end of the chapter. While there are times when a signal generated by this idea does not work, we tend to make serious gains when it works, especially when we are willing to let our winners run.

Trading Examples

Spreads are not considered in these examples. The vertical red line on the left shows where a trade was entered and the vertical red line on the right shows where a trade was exited.

Example 1:

We would like to show the first trading example on the EUR/CAD. In Figure 3, from February to March 2014, the price was above the level at 1.5000. Starting from April 2014, the price began to weaken, which made it break the horizontal line at 1.5000 to the downside. At the same time, the EMA 10 was sloping downwards. The crossing of the horizontal line to the downside signalled an opportunity to go short. The trade was taken and the target was hit after a few months.

F3) Horizontal Line at 1.5000 Breached to the Downside

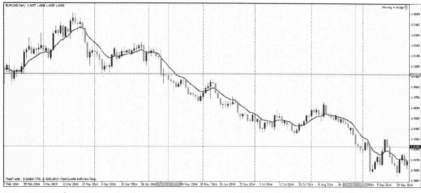

The EUR/CAD price began to weaken, which made it break the horizontal line at 1.5000 to the downside.

Instrument: EUR/CAD
Order: Sell
Entry date: 13 May 2014
Entry price: 1.4950
Stop loss: 1.5150
Take profit: 1.4350
Exit date: 27 August 2014
Profit/loss: 600 pips

Example 2:

Here is another example on the USD/JPY, which reinforces the way this strategy works. In Figure 4, in the USD/JPY daily chart, we saw an opportunity to go long when the horizontal line at the great psychological level of 100.00 was broken to the upside, as the EMA 10 was sloping upwards. A long position was initiated and the price moved seriously upwards, nearly reaching the target. However, in January 2014, the price began to drop considerably, and it generally consolidated till August 2014, when a very strong bullish movement resumed. Our target was reached and even far exceeded, for the price moved upwards by over 900 pips since the long position was initiated. In the chart, the candlesticks were made smaller to give a better depiction of the trade.

F4) A Long Term Bullish Signal on the USD/JPY

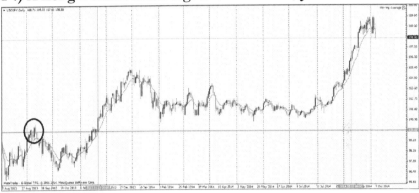

The USD/JPY daily chart.

Instrument: USD/JPY
Order: Buy
Entry date: 21 November 2013
Entry price: 100.15
Stop loss: 98.15
Take profit: 106.15
Exit date: 9 September 2014
Profit/loss: 600 pips

Many traders do not have the patience to let a profitable position like this run. We can see that in spite of desperate attempts by the bears, the price has failed to even test the great psychological level at 100.00, let alone breach it to the downside. Most traders would have exited the order in January 2014 when the bearish retracement began, and they would have done that with a good profit (despite the fact that the target was not reached). Even if the great level at 100.00 was tested, the position would have been smoothed at breakeven. Look at the oval shape on the chart. Sometimes, the horizontal line can be tested as a result of the bullish pressure, but the price would fail to breach it to the upside. This does not make us go short automatically, because the bullish attempt failed. We cannot just perform the opposite of the logic in order to improve the gains, for it would be like doing brain surgery with an axe.

Conclusion

When a significant support or resistance level that has at least three zeros is breached to the downside or the upside, there might be a continuation of that powerful force for a long period of time. The same is true for four zeros. This speculation idea makes us look for position trading opportunities and be responsible after we take advantage of the opportunities. Trading is a career that demands our responsibility. Any field of thought that blames the markets for what traders experience is an irrational field of thought. However, the trading opportunities that come from this method are few and far between, so it may be added to the strategies we currently use. We are soldiers of the financial markets, and we have been generously rewarded for our willingness to take risks.

Strategy Snapshot	
Strategy Name:	Round Numbers Trading Method
Strategy Type:	Trend-following
Suitability:	Good for part-time traders
Trading Style:	Position trading
Time Horizon:	Daily charts
Indicators:	The Horizontal Line and the EMA 10
Price Levels:	Round numbers, especially the ones ending in three or four zeros
Bullish Setup:	When an important level is breached upwards and the EMA 10 is normally trending upwards, we go long (sometimes on bearish retracements)
Bearish Setup:	When an important level is breached downwards and the EMA 10 is normally trending downwards, we go short (sometimes on bullish retracements)
Position Size:	Please use 0.01 lots for each $2,000
Stop Loss:	200 pips
Take Profit:	600 pips
Risk to Reward Ratio:	1:3
Breakeven Stop:	You can set your stop at breakeven after a gain of about 100 pips
Exit:	When the stop, or the breakeven stop, or the take profit is hit

When to Buy or Sell on Smaller Time Horizons

A Solution to the Trader's Dilemma

Intraday traders prefer to speculate on short term or medium term price movements. Now, the most frequently asked question is "should I buy or sell?" This is a trader's dilemma: the inability to decide whether one should buy long or sell short. Therefore, there are factors you need to consider before you take a temporary position. For instance, no matter what time horizon you choose, the predominant bias will impact your positions. Taking trades while making sure that the dominant bias favours your direction can give you a huge edge. This chapter explains one way of doing just that.

The Trader's Dilemma – Should I buy or Sell?

Janet likes to speculate on 30 minute charts, for that is what fits her mind set. She does not like to hold a position for more than a few days at most. She would even prefer to open new orders and close them within one day (or two days). She looks at the USD/CHF on a 30-minute chart, but she is a kind of afraid to open new trades. According to her past experience, the market may turn against her once she opens a new trade. She does not know why this sometimes happens. Yesterday on the USD/CHF, everything looked OK for a short trade order, but no sooner had she opened a short order than the pair rallied massively, moving by over 120 pips that day. That is why she is sceptical about her decision to go long on the pair today. Janet needs to find a way of making trading decision on her favourite 30-minute charts with confidence.

Janet is not alone. A trader opens a position and soon, the market is going against that position. The position may even get stopped out before the market begins to move in the expected direction. Why? Because as mentioned in the introduction to this chapter, no matter the time horizon you choose, the predominant bias will have an impact on your positions. When you get a bearish signal on a 15-minute chart and you sell without looking at a higher time horizon, you may be adversely affected, especially if the price direction on the 1-hour chart is bullish. It would mean that what you see as a 'sell' signal on the 30-minute chart is a mere pullback in the context of an uptrend in higher time frames. This is a trap that can be avoided.

Getting Favoured by the Dominant Biases

When financial media squawks about going against the yen, which has been sensible in the face of the recent bears' domination, things would come to a point when bulls are no longer going long in the market. When the bears dominate, do you think the bulls would continue purchasing at a loss? This is also true when most analysts prefer a strong USD/GBP (Cable). When most speculators go long because they want the Cable to appreciate (something that has been holding true in recent times) the bulls cannot bank their profits if they refuse to smooth their positions. They smooth against the masses' expectation that invariably prefer to join a trend when it has gone too far. The masses are usually caught on the wrong side of the market.

Then, it is better for intraday traders to make sure that what they are doing agrees with the real medium term trend in a particular market. For instance, when there is a 'buy' signal on the USD/CHF on three time horizons, say 15-minute, 30-minute and 1-hour charts (as used in this strategy), the trader's confidence is increased, knowing well that she/he is going in the normal direction of the market, though there is no certainty. In a southward trend, if three time horizons agree with one another, it means that there are active and passionate speculators in the market. It is not because they want to push the price against the origin of the current movement; it is because they want to capitalize on the current imbalance in the price. This reveals that the Smart Money has opened large positions at the current moment, so that the imbalance in the price can be taken advantage of. Should the price start plummeting at this time, the southward trend would continue, making lower highs and lower lows.

Though it may be used round the clock, this strategy works best during London and US sessions. In addition, profitability increases on Tuesdays, Wednesdays and Thursdays, but it works on Mondays and Fridays as well. We need to know what is happening on our charts. There are immense riches in the markets only if we know how to tap them. Many people are not aware of this. The Strategy Snapshot at the end of the chapter gives for further details on how to use this trading method. You should follow the system mechanically, removing emotions from your approach, then you should witness an increase in your portfolio balance.

The indicator used is the Simple Moving Average (SMA) period 10, which also enables you to catch a wave early enough. Moving averages are great for trend identification. When the price crosses the SMA 10 to the upside or to the downside on all the time horizons, a short term or a medium term bullish or bearish signal is confirmed. Note that we are talking about a short-term or a medium term signal, not a long term one. This is the reason why we would not go for more than 100 pips per trade.

Some Past Trades

You should not speculate on a pair or cross whose spread is more than 10 pips. Spreads are not taken into consideration in the examples below. Please remember this: if there are bullish signals only on two time horizons, we would never take the trade. We want our signal to be confirmed on all the three time horizons. The red vertical line on the 15-minute chart shows where a trade is entered in agreement with the other higher time horizons, since the 15-minute chart serves as the point of entry. Once you enter with a position, you should not be disturbed by ensuing fleeting upswings and downswings in price; just stick to your entry, trade management and exit rules.

Example A

On 11 December 2013, the AUD/USD was bearish (weak) as evident on the 1-hour chart (Figure 1) and 30-minute chart (Figure 2). The bears' domination was confirmed on the two aforementioned charts, and the 15-minute chart (Figure 3) also gave the same bearish signal on the AUD/ USD. That meant it was utterly foolish to buy the pair at that moment: the best choice was to go short. A short trade was opened and it transpired as shown below.

F1) A Sell Signal on the 1-Hour Chart

AUD/USD: A bearish signal on the 1-hour chart. Price crossed the SMA 10 to the downside, giving a bearish signal.

F2) A Sell Signal on 30-Minute Chart

AUD/USD: A bearish signal on the 30-minute chart. Price crossed the SMA 10 to the downside, giving a bearish signal to confirm what the 1-hour chart was showing.

F3) A Sell Signal on the 15-Minute Chart – a Point of entry

AUD/USD: A sell signal on the 15-minute chart. Price crossed the SMA 10 to the downside, giving a bearish signal to confirm what both the 1-hour and the 30-minute charts were showing. It is helpful to take signals in the direction of higher time horizons.

Instrument: AUD/USD
Order: Sell
Entry date: 11 December, 2013
Entry price: 0.9135
Stop loss: 0.9185
Take profit: 0.9035
Exit date: 12 December, 2013
Profit/loss: 100 pips

Example B

In Figure 4, three GBP/JPY time horizons, 15-min, 30-min and 1-hr, are put on the chart. This makes it far easier to watch the three time horizons at the same time, while making informed trading decisions. On 13 December 2013, the price of the GBP/JPY, which was sliding southward, crossed the SMA 10 on the three time horizons respectively. Once this action was confirmed on the 1-hr and 30-min charts, the signal was taken off the 15-min chart. It was a profitable trade.

F4) Sell Confirmation on GBP/JPY

The price of the GBP/JPY crossed the SMA 10 on the three time horizons respectively.

Instrument: GBP/JPY
Order: Sell
Entry date: 13 December 2013
Entry price: 169.20
Stop loss: 169.70
Take profit: 168.20
Exit date: 13 December 2013
Profit/loss: 100 pips

Taking a Partial Profit on Meta Trader 4 (MT4)

In order to avoid premature exits owing to maniacal swings in price, trailing stops are not recommended for this strategy. Another reason is the relatively tight stops. When an open trade has gone in your favour by more than 50 pips, you may move your stop to break-even (adjust your entry price to be equal to your initial stop). Then you may close about 30 to 50 per cent of the trade while you ride the remaining trade size until your target is possibly hit.

In most cases, this was possible on MT4 until recently. You would just right-click on an open trade and choose 'Close Order.' Then you input the lot size for the partial trade you wanted to close, and click the bar below, whose colour depended on whether the trade was long or short. Part of the trade would be closed with profit or loss, when the remaining trade size would still be open in the market.

Unfortunately, the latest versions of MT4 no longer have this unique function, except certain brokers that still support it. It may be possible if your broker allows it; so check with your broker. Without the feature mentioned above, the general trick is to simply open two positions on the same trade. Let us say you trade 1 lot in general. Then depending on your preferences you can open two positions: for example if you want to close 30 per cent in the event of a 50-pip gain you will open one trade 0.3 lots and one 0.7 lots. In another instance, if your portfolio is worth $1000 and you use 0.1 lots, you may want to open two trades with 0.05 lots each, (whereas 0.05 + 0.05 = 0.1). Should you prefer to close 50 per cent of the trade after gaining 50 pips, you would just close one of your dual positions, after you have set stops to breakeven on both.

Your Momentary Loss Does Not Mean You Are Not a Good Trader

The trading method works both in bull and bear markets. It can allow us to harvest gains, though it may sometimes generate signals that cause negativity. By sticking to the lot sizes, entry, stops, target rules and other recommendations, we are bound to face occasional negativity triumphantly. We are no longer immature traders – we have come a long way. Someone may want to deny the merit of trading when losing. You may be having a drawdown, yet you are an expert trader. You may have five or ten consecutive losses and still be one of the best traders in the world. I can lose all my trades in a week or a month and still tell you that trading is one of the best jobs in the world. We are happy when we lose and when we gain. It is even psychologically dangerous to always win without losing from time to time.

Conclusion

This piece shows you how to wait for a signal on a smaller time horizon that agrees with higher time horizons. In order to go in the direction which the market favours, you need to pinpoint them on other time horizons as well. You do not need magical power or supernatural ability to be victorious in the markets. You simply need to ensure that you go in the direction the market favours. This method is not perfect, but it is powerful. While you experience the pleasure of trading, do not forget that your momentary loss does not mean you are not a good trader.

Strategy Snapshot	
Strategy Name:	Medium-term Trend Trader
Strategy Type:	Day Trading
Suitability:	Good for full-time traders
Time Horizons:	15-minute charts, 30-minute charts and 1-hour charts
Indicator:	SMA period 10
Long Entry Rule:	Price crosses the SMA 10 on 15-min, 30-min and 1-hr charts to the upside. Often the 15-minute chart would be the point of entry while the other time horizons would confirm the direction of the market
Short Entry Rule:	price crosses the SMA 10 on 15-min, 30-min and 1-hr charts to the downside. Often the 15-minute chart would be the point of entry while the other time horizons would confirm the direction of the market
Stop:	50 pips
Target:	100 pips
Position Sizing:	0.01 lots for each $1000
Risk per Trade:	0.5%
Risk to Reward Ratio:	1:2
Trade management:	See the section titled 'Taking a Partial Profit on Meta Trader 4'
Maximum trades:	5 trades per day
Duration:	40 hours maximum

A Forex Freedom Strategy

Swing and Position Trading for Part-time Traders

When we look at a chart, we should ask ourselves some honest questions before making a trading decision. Some of the crucial questions are these: What direction would Smart Money want to take? How do they survive the markets by taking this approach? How can we then become successful while using that approach? This chapter answers these questions and arrives at a useful trading approach.

Determining the Validity of a Bias or its Reversal

A winning approach is the one that takes advantage of the prevailing trend in a subtle way. Doing so can be easier than imagined. When a trend is seen on a medium-term or a long-term time frame, one would need to ensure that the trend is valid before one makes a decision. For example, when you look at a daily chart and see a downtrend, would you conclude that you could make money by trading it? Or when you look at a 4-hour chart and see an uptrend, would you conclude that you could make money by trading it?

A daily chart may show a long-term downtrend, but a protracted bullish reversal may have already started forming. This bullish reversal may later translate into a dominant uptrend, but such a change would be reflected first on a smaller time frame, because it takes time for a change to be reflected on a higher time frame. Alternatively, a reversal on a smaller time frame may just be a fleeting experience that traps some noobs into thinking that the budding bias has been rubberstamped.

Following a market crash when speculators ought to buy fear in order to ride the ensuing bull markets, they rather flee, thinking they can only buy confidence later. While some large-hearted investors make orders for the long term, others prefer short-term moves, scalping and taking profits along the way. They might later spend the gains on bottles of beer.

What determines the bias of a currency trading instrument is the expectation of the majority of the speculators, not always the economic figures. Negative economic figures may only have transitory effect if the majority of the speculators think the price is still great for the bulls. How can we know whether a trend is currently valid or whether a reversal is a decoy or an opportunity? We can see clearly when the chart depicts the tail end of a precarious trend or the confirmation of a trend. However, we want to know the direction the winning traders might take, plus how she/he moves ahead by managing risk and eventually becomes successful by making average profit that is larger than average loss.

The Forex Freedom Strategy Explained

To start with, we would look at a highly trending market, whose trend is vivid (in the same direction) in the daily chart and the 4-hour chart. Place a 30-period SMA (Simple Moving Average) in the daily chart to show the long-term trend. Place a 20-period SMA in the 4-hour chart to show the medium-term trend, which must agree with the long-term trend on the daily chart. This means that as the SMA 30 on the daily chart confirms a bias, the SMA 20 on the 4-hour chart must also confirm the same bias. As you probably know, the purpose of the SMA is to help determine the major bias in a chart. The period of the SMA on the daily is different from the period of the SMA on the 4-hour chart – this enables us to handle the vagaries of the market deftly.

Put the Stochastic Oscillator, default parameters, in the hourly-chart (of the same instrument) to show the short-term movement. With this, you want to buy long when the price enters into the oversold territory – buying when an instrument is on sale, and in the context of an uptrend. There are many uses for the Stochastic Oscillator, but the most common one is to buy long when it saunters into the oversold territory and sell short when it saunters into the overbought territory.

The overbought territory is the territory above the level 80 and the oversold territory is the level below 20. But in order to improve the effectiveness of the Stochastic, we would buy only when it drops below the level 10 and sell only when it goes above the level 90. Movements below the level 10 and above the level 90 are less frequent and more reliable for reversal signals than the movements below the level 20 and above the level 80. With the Stochastic in the hourly chart, we are not interested in buying and selling automatically when there are signals from the indicator. Instead of this, we want to consider the signals that agree with the confirmed bias on the 4-hour chart and on the daily chart, since the correction that triggers a signal on the Stochastic is the same action that enables us to go along with the dominant bias as the price becomes more attractive. When the Stochastic generates a signal that goes contrary to the confirmed bias on the 4-hour chart and the daily chart, the signal is disregarded.

Convincing Setups in the Charts

The first convincing setup example was taken on the EUR/AUD chart. In Figure 1, you can see the cross in a clean long-term downtrend, punctuated by occasional short lived rallies. The red vertical line in the chart simply shows the day a short trade was opened on the EUR/AUD 1-hour chart. The SMA 30 was sloping downwards.

F1) The Downward EUR/AUD on the Daily Chart

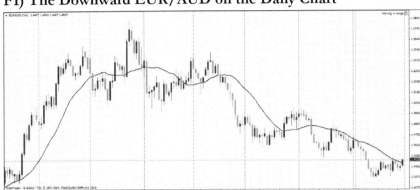

You can see the cross in a clean long-term downtrend, punctuated by occasional short lived rallies.

Likewise on the EUR/AUD 4-hour chart, the SMA 20 was sloping downwards (Figure 2). The chart was also punctuated by short-term rallies. The red vertical line in the chart simply shows the day a short trade was opened on the EUR/AUD 1-hour chart. On both the daily chart and the 4-hour chart, the SMAs 30 and 20 are in blue colour.

F2) The Downward EUR/AUD on the 4-Hour Chart

On the EUR/AUD 4-hour chart, the SMA 20 is sloping downwards.

In Figure 3, the Stochastic Oscillator went overbought (above the level 90) on the hourly chart. On the hourly chart, we are not concerned whether the market is bullish or bearish; we are only concerned about the indicator going into an overbought territory as opposed to the dominant downtrend on the daily chart and the 4-hour chart. This offers a low risk and high reward entry. We should note that when the Stochastic enters the extreme levels of ten or 90, it gets corrected quickly. Therefore a quick action is required when this condition is met. On 3 June 2014, immediately after the Stochastic was overbought, a short trade was opened and it became a roaring success.

F3) The EUR/AUD on the Hourly Chart

The Stochastic Oscillator went overbought (above the level 90) on the hourly chart.

Instrument: EUR/AUD
Order: Sell
Entry date: 3 June 2014
Entry price: 1.4720
Stop-loss: 1.4870
Trailing stop: 1.4570
Take profit: 1.4420
Exit date: 11 June 2014
Exit price: 1.4420
Status: Closed
Profit/loss: 300 pips

In this last example, the AUD/ USD is shown in Figure 4 on the daily chart, the 4-hour chart and the hourly chart. This enables you to monitor the three charts with more ease. On 11 March 2014, the Stochastic went into an oversold territory, showing that the AUD/USD was being sold heavily when the dominant trend was bullish. Prior to the time that the Stochastic went into the oversold region (giving a buy signal) it had already been seen that the SMA 30 was sloping upwards in the daily chart and that the SMA 20 was sloping upwards in the 4-hour chart. It is the slope that mattered at that time, not whether the price was above or below the SMA. As soon as the long order was opened, the market went upwards with magnanimous alacrity.

F4) The AUD/USD on Daily, 4-Hour and Hourly Charts

On 11 March 2014, the Stochastic went into an oversold territory, showing that the AUD/USD was being sold heavily when the dominant trend was bullish.

Instrument: AUD/USD
Order: Buy
Entry date: 11 March 2014
Entry price: 0.8965
Stop-loss: 0.8815
Trailing stop: 0.9115
Take profit: 0.9265
Exit date: 28 March 2014

Exit price: 0.9265
Status: Closed
Profit/loss: 300 pips

Conclusion

As simple as this strategy may be, it should only be enjoyed by the trader with commendable mettle. You should take care only to trade Forex instruments that usually move very well. In a nutshell, don't trade instruments that usually do not move very well or have a great deal of uncertainty. You would see these instruments as they move constantly sideways in the charts or as they are highly volatile without following a predominant course. These are some of the unsexy markets you should try to avoid. When the rules of the game are understood and adhered to, the ultimate rewards would be agreeable to the mind. Better is the conclusion of a matter than the beginning thereof.

Strategy Snapshot	
Strategy Name:	Forex Freedom Strategy
Strategy Type:	Swing/position trading
Suitability:	Great for part-time traders
Indicators:	SMA 30 and 20 (colour blue), Stochastic Oscillator (default parameters) levels 90 and 10
Time Horizons:	The daily chart, the 4-hour chart and the hourly chart
Bullish Setup:	SMA 30 upwards in the daily chart, SMA 20 upwards in the 4-hour chart and the Stochastic extremely oversold (below the level 10) in the hourly chart
Bearish Setup:	SMA 30 downwards in the daily chart, SMA 20 downwards in the 4-hour chart and the Stochastic extremely overbought (above the level 90) in the hourly chart
Stop:	150 pips from the entry price
Target:	300 pips from the entry price
Risk per Trade:	1%
Risk to Reward Ratio:	1:2
Break-Even Stop:	You can adjust your stop to break-even after you have gained up to 100 pips
Trailing Stop:	You can set a 50% trailing stop after you have gained up to 200 pips
Exit Rules:	Either the stop is hit, the break-even stop is hit, the trailing stop is hit, the target is hit or the trade is closed after the maximum duration expires
Maximum Trade Duration:	4 weeks

A Demand and Supply Trading Method

Buy Low, Sell High

As we experience the zigs and zags of trading, we want to be sure that we are doing the right thing. Doing the right thing means going with the flow of the markets. At a demand zone, buyers are willing to buy from sellers who are rushing into the imbalance of the price at a wrong time. The same thing is true of a supply zone: the sellers want to sell to the buyers who want to go long when the imbalance in the price is against them. This kind of timing can scupper the effort of speculators who go into the wrong side of the market. The demand and supply trading method makes you buy logically low and sell logically high, and do it right.

The Trading Method Requires Seriousness

The trading method detailed here requires seriousness on the part of the speculator. Trading is a serious business. Anything you spend your time, energy and resources on for the purpose of profit is business. Any activity you rigorously engage yourself in for the purpose of making profit is business. Whatever costs you nothing will bring nothing to you in return. You do not need to go to Harvard to know what business is.

Getting familiar with subtle patterns in the charts will enable you to know what to do in any circumstances brought about by the markets. The logic behind the method has been alluded to in the introduction to this chapter. In order to understand it better, we would say that a price that is caught in a bearish correction may rally when it reaches a zone of previous support (demand zone). A price that rallies massively may be challenged at a previous resistance (supply zone). A sideways market tends to result in a breakout, as a directional movement occurs. The directional movement tends to become significant. Those who know how to play this simple market pattern will surely attain a helpful insight into the real direction of the line of the least resistance. These are exactly what we are looking for in the charts. We want to know where the price may rally after testing an area of previous support and where it may plummet after testing an area of previous resistance.

What we want to do is to anticipate those potential turning points and place pending orders around those vivid demand and supply levels so that our orders may be filled when prices reach those levels. We should set our stop-loss and take-profit levels before we open the pending orders (which are only buy-limit and sell-limit orders). We should also set the date of expiration, which is usually one month in duration, if we speculate on 4-hour charts, so that the pending order could be automatically liquidated in case our order is not filled within one month.

Locating Demand and Supply Zones in Charts

You need to use discretion as well as patience in pinpointing demand and supply zones. Primarily, the focus is on 4-hour charts, but daily charts can also be used, especially when it seems the demand and supply zones on a 4-hour chart do not appear strong enough. The higher the time frame, the more important are the zones. The horizontal lines in the charts depict the areas of demand and supply zones. Let us look at Figure 1.

F1) A Demand Zone on the AUD/JPY

On 3 February 2014, after the price tested the previous support (demand zone), the correction was rejected at a low of 88.51.

We can see what happened on 3 February 2014 after the price tested the previous support (demand zone). More study of the chart shows that the prior trend was bearish. The correction was rejected at a low of 88.51. Price rallied a bit and got corrected to the downside. When the previous support was tested again, the price went out of balance, making it impossible to go lower. The price then rallied conspicuously. The point here is that a pending order could have been set before the price reached the demand zone, so that our order could be triggered whether we are present or not.

Short trades may be sought or long trades may be sought, depending on your expectation. If you are left on your own, could you locate potential demand and supply zones? You are provided with a naked GBP/CAD chart. See Figure 2. There are clean demand and supply zones in the chart. Could you locate them? If you could, congratulations!

F2) Try to Locate Demand and Supply Zones Here

There are clean demand and supply zones in this naked GBP/CAD 4-chart.

For those who cannot locate the potential demand and supply zones in that chart, the answers are provided for you in Figure 3. You can see that, although the overall bias seems bearish, there are significant upswings and downswings in the market. When the market reached a high of 1.8610 (a supply zone) on 10 March 2014 and then dropped conspicuously, a sell-limit pending order was opened in case the price reverted back to the previous supply zone. The price actually did that, and our pending order was triggered, reaching our target of 200 pips in less than seven trading days.

F3) Actual Demand and Supply Zones on the GBP/CAD 4-Hour Chart

When the market reached a high of 1.8610 (a supply zone) in 10 March 2014 and then dropped conspicuously, a sell-limit pending order was opened in case the price reverted back to the previous supply zone.

There is also another potential demand zone at 1.8312. That zone was created on 6 March 2014. The GBP/CAD challenged that demand zone on 18 March 2014, making desperate effort to breach it to the downside. Since there were more willing buyers than sellers at that zone, further downside move was rejected and the cross rallied significantly and hit the 200-pip target on the following day.

A Trading Example on a Daily Chart

As it is mentioned above, it is possible to use this trading method on daily charts as well. If there are no convincing demand and supply zones on a 4-hour chart, you may want to switch to a daily chart. You must bear in mind that the demand and supply zones on the daily chart are more significant than all the time frames lower than it. The price moves on the daily chart are also more significant than the time frames lower than it, and therefore you may want to increase your stop to 150 or 200 pips. The take profit can be increased to 300 or 400 pips. The trading duration could also be increased to two or three months.

In this particular example of a daily chart, a trade was triggered on the NZD/USD on 31 January 2014. In Figure 4, a price low (demand zone) was identified. That is an area where the bears are determined to resist further bearish moves in the market. A pending order was placed around that zone. After two months the order was triggered when the price plunged and tested that zone. It was a successful trade. Here the entry date is given as the date when the pending order was triggered, not when it was placed. The entry price was the low of the day when the potential demand level was identified discretionally (29 November 2014).

F4) Demand Zone on the NZD/USD Daily Chart

A trade was triggered on the NZD/USD on 31 January 2014.

Instrument: NZD/USD
Order: Buy limit
Entry date: 31 January 2014
Entry price: 0.8083
Stop-loss: 0.7883
Take profit: 0.8484
Profit: 400 pips
Status: Closed

The price was still in an uptrend at the time of the preparation of this chapter. Since our order was triggered, the price has moved so far by over 560 pips. Sometimes, the market may not test the previous supply and demand zone before it continues its journey according to the established bias.

Conclusion

If the concept of objective demand and supply zones in the charts is new to you, you may want to practice with this trading method in simulation mode until it becomes second nature. While doing this, do not seek perfection or set 'too' high standards. We do not always need to wait for perfect market conditions before we place our pending orders.

A farmer who waits until conditions are perfect may never sow seed or reap his harvest. Of course, high standards are commendable. Sometimes, though, we may set standards so high that we invite disappointment and failure. A newbie learning the art of trading, for example, must be prepared to make mistakes, aware that he will learn from these. A perfectionist, however, would likely shudder at the thought of making orders that may be inaccurate – an attitude that will impede his progress. How much better is it to be modest in our expectations!

Strategy Snapshot	
Strategy Name:	Demand and Supply Trading Method
Strategy Type:	Position trading
Trading Style:	Discretionary
Suitability:	Good for part-time traders
Time Horizons:	4-hour charts, sometimes daily charts
Order Type:	Pending orders (buy limit and sell limit)
Entry Rules:	Based on powerful demand and supply zones on the charts
Stop-Loss:	100 pips (150-200 pips on daily charts)
Take Profit:	200 pips (300-400 pips in daily charts)
Position Sizing:	Please use 0.01 lots for each $1000 (and thus making it 0.1 lots for $10,000); or 1.0 lots for each $100,000
Risk per Trade:	1%
Risk to Reward Ratio:	1:2
Break-Even:	You can move your stop to break-even after you gain up to 70 pips
Trailing Stop:	You can set up to a 50% trailing stop after you have gained up to 170 pips
Maximum Signals:	20 signals
Maximum Trades:	10 trades per month
Maximum Trade Duration:	One month (3-4 months on daily charts)

A Parabolic SAR Trading Method

Trading the Short Term Trending Movements

There are many ways to make money in the markets. We are talking about speculators who have a huge edge because of their knowledge and risk control methods. One of the ways to make money is explained here. It has to do with one great, but often underestimated indicator called Parabolic SAR. The indicator is very helpful when it is used properly in the markets. How can we use the Parabolic SAR properly and thus get rewarded financially? This chapter answers the question.

The Behaviour of the Parabolic SAR

The Parabolic SAR is useful in knowing where to put stop-loss and where to trail the stop when the market moves in our direction. When the indicator appears below the price, it generates a long signal (reverse the rationale for when it appears above the price). When the Parabolic SAR appears in the opposite direction, then an exit is generated. Since the indicator follows a dominant bias, we can say it is a trend-following indicator. When a trending movement begins, the indicator follows it (acting like a trailing stop). This means that when the trading instrument goes upwards, the Parabolic SAR which acts as a stop rises logically with it as long as the bias is upwards. When the trading instrument goes downwards, the Parabolic SAR which acts as a stop goes down logically with it as long as the bias is downwards.

In the wake of an uptrend, the Parabolic SAR continues to rise in a bullish market and thus guards our gains as the bullish market continues. When we follow this analytical tool, we can see the reason why it would not be in our best interest to widen our stop. When the trend reverses drastically and crosses the Parabolic SAR downwards, that means the bias has gone bearish and thus, the indicator shows above the price. As the market backtracks, the indicator begins to act as a trailing stop for the bearish market – as long as the bearish market holds out. Since the Parabolic SAR does not go up in a bearish market, it guards our profits in the market. The same is true of a bullish market; the indicator does not go down in a bullish market, and thus it protects our profits, ensuring that we get out only when there is a considerable change in the bias. This feature is useful for those who use the indicator as a trailing stop. In this chapter, the Parabolic SAR is used mainly in the entry criteria.

Combining the Parabolic SAR with the ADX Period 14

The Parabolic SAR works great in a trending move, so we may consider putting it aside when the market is not trending. Otherwise, the accuracy of the signals generated by the indicator may be reduced considerably in flat markets. It is irrational to use the indicator in a trendless market. Those who fail to resist the irrational urge pay a heavy price. That being said, a trendless market is a trap for Parabolic SAR users. Only time will tell whether it is the trap or the squirrel that will survive on the farm. How do we know that the market is flat (trendless)? We know this simply by looking at the chart and seeing that the price is generally moving sideways. How do we know that the market is trending? We know this simply by looking at the chart, and seeing that the price is going upwards or going downwards. Moreover, the Average Directional Movement Index (ADX) period

14 can also help us to know when the bears dominate the market or when the bulls dominate. This happens when the ADX +DI crosses above the –DI; or vice versa. +DI signifies bullish pressure and –DI signifies bearish pressure. Combining this with the Parabolic SAR improves the trading accuracy in a trending market.

You can see the Strategy Snapshot for entry criteria for short and long trades. When a trading signal is being taken, we want to be sure that the Parabolic SAR on the hourly chart and 15-minute chart are saying the same thing. Do not enter a trade against the 15-minute parabolic SAR.

Some Recent Trades

The colour for the Parabolic SAR, which appears as dots in the chart, has been changed to blue. The ADX period 14 line has been changed to green. The +DI is blue while the –DI is red. The ADX level 30 is chosen (black). A bias is particularly strong when the ADX line goes above the level 30. Please note that these are not the default colours: The ones used are the ones the author preferred. In the examples below, the red vertical line on the left shows where a trade was entered, and the red vertical line on the right shows where it was smoothed, especially in the hourly charts. We do not consider spreads here.

Example 1:

On 26 August 2014, the EUR/CAD, which was already bearish in outlook, continued its weakness. In Figure 1, you can see the Parabolic SAR and the ADX period 14 in the hourly chart. A sell signal was generated as the Parabolic SAR appeared above the price, and soon after, the signal was confirmed by the ADX as the –DI crossed the +DI to the upside. Seeing this, the 15-minute chart of the same trading instrument was checked and it was seen that the Parabolic SAR in that chart was also giving the same sell signal (at the same time and the same hour as the hourly chart). The trade was taken immediately. The only thing that mattered was the position of the Parabolic SAR in the 15-minute chart, confirming the signal that was seen in the hourly chart. After this, what happened to the Parabolic SAR – whether it appeared next above or below the price – was of no significance. It was a high probability setup, which turned out to be a winning trade. This kind of trading approach enables low-risk entries plus optimal stops.

F1) A Sell Signal on the EUR/CAD

The Parabolic SAR and the ADX period 14 in the hourly chart.

Instrument: EUR/CAD
Order: Sell
Entry date: 26 August 2014
Entry price: 1.4465
Stop-loss: 1.4505
Take profit: 1.4360
Exit date: 27 August 2014
Status: Closed
Profit/loss: 80 pips

Figure 2 shows the 15-minute chart that confirmed the signal when the Parabolic SAR appeared above the price, as shown by the oval in the chart. The bearish trend continued after that as you can see. The ADX is not necessary in the 15-minute chart.

F2) The Parabolic SAR in the 15-Minute Chart

The 15-minute chart that confirmed the signal when the Parabolic SAR appeared above the price, as shown by the oval in the chart.

Example 2:

On the same day that the short trade on the EUR/CAD was taken, there was a buy signal on the CAD/JPY. The Parabolic SAR appeared below the price. Then this was confirmed by the ADX period 14, whose +DI crossed the –DI to the upside. You can see this in Figure 3. During the course of the long trade, the ADX line went above the level 30 (black line): it even went above the level 70 because the bullish bias had a lot of stamina in it. The trade was opened and it reached the target level. Immediately the target level was reached, the trade was closed automatically; or how long does the blinking of an eye take?

F3) A Buy Signal on the CAD/JPY

On the same day that the short trade on the EUR/CAD was taken, there was a buy signal on the CAD/JPY.

Figure 4 shows how the bullish trading signal that was generated in the CAD/JPY hourly chart was confirmed by the position of the Parabolic SAR in the CAD/JPY 15-minute chart. This happened at the same time and at the same hour. Of course, it is possible to fit the hourly chart and the 15-minute chart into a single window (or figure), but they are shown separately here for the purpose of clarity.

F4) The Parabolic SAR in the 15-Minute Chart

The bullish trading signal that was generated in the CAD/JPY hourly chart was confirmed by the position of the Parabolic SAR in the CAD/JPY 15-minute chart.

Instrument: CAD/JPY
Order: Buy
Entry date: 26 August 2014
Entry price: 94.70
Stop-loss: 94.30
Take profit: 95.50
Exit date: 27 August 2014
Status: Closed
Profit/loss: 80 pips

As mentioned in the Strategy Snapshot at the end of the chapter, we exit a trade only when the stop or the target (take profit) is hit, or after the maximum trading duration. While the two indicators are used to generate entry signals, they are not used at all in generating exit signals. This means that we no longer care about the positions of the indicators after our entry rules have been fulfilled in the hourly chart and the 15-minute chart. Moreover, we would not widen the stop, or run our loss under any circumstances. It is an irrational feeling that makes us think that we need to run a loss with the hope that it can come back to our entry price.

Traders are unwise to give in to that poisonous emotion.

Conclusion

This trading approach is great for intraday and swing traders; though the rules coming with it must be followed religiously. Sometimes, things go contrary to our fear. In the past, we may have experienced some negativity because we fail to take some prudent measures in our trading approach; or because we take some illogical measures. We must trade with the strategy flawlessly, since we do not know which trade would bring us the desired profits. Our courage and determination to focus on our trading goals grow stronger through challenges. We thought that we would be giving a lot of ourselves, but in actuality, we would be gaining so much more.

Strategy Snapshot	
Strategy Name:	Parabolic SAR Trading Method
Strategy Type:	Trend-following
Suitability:	Good for intraday and swing traders
Time Horizon 1:	Hourly charts
Time Horizon 2:	15-minute chart (for confirming entry signals)
Indicator 1:	Parabolic SAR (default parameters)
Indicator 2:	Average Directional Movement Index (ADX) period 14
Short Entry:	Go short when the Parabolic SAR appears above the price and the ADX 14 has its +DI below the –DI. At this time, the SAR in the 15-minute chart must also be above the price
Long Entry:	Go long when the Parabolic SAR appears below the price and the ADX 14 has its –DI below the +DI. At this time, the SAR in the 15-minute chart must also be below the price
Exit:	A trade is closed only when the stop or the target is hit. It is also closed if it is still open after 48 hours
Filter 1:	Stop trading for the week when your loss exceeds 3.5%. But so long as you do not lose 3.5%, you may want to trade continuously
Filter 2:	Do not trade a sideways market. Only trade a trending market
Filter 3:	Do not trade against the 15-minute Parabolic SAR. Take a trade only when it agrees with the 15-minute Parabolic SAR
Position Size:	Use 0.01 lots for each $2000 (and thus making it 0.05 lots for $10,000); or 0.1 lots for each 20,000 cents in a cent account (making it 0.5 lots for each 100,000 cents)
Stop:	40 pips

Take Profit:	80 pips
Trailing Stop:	Trailing stop is optional – it may be used according to the movement of Parabolic SAR
Maximum Trade Duration:	Close an open trade that is more than 48 hours old

Harnessing Profits from Popular Fundamentals

A News Trading Strategy in Forex

Speculating on key fundamentals can leave you with decent gains, providing that you know how to do that exactly. Trying to harness profits from the impact created by popular economic figures has its own risk as well as its own reward. Luckily, with guided rules and risk control parameters, the high volatility that follows the release of economic figures like the ones described here can be capitalised on. As some neophytes are whacked with losses or rewarded with gains, you would do well to be in control of what happens to your account during strong economic figures release. Here is one trading method that can be employed in dealing with key fundamentals affecting the markets, especially the ones that most traders anticipate.

Fundamental Figures Can Have an Effect on the Market

When major fundamental figures are released, the trading world feels the impact. Sometimes the figures may push the markets in the direction of the primary trend, or contrary to it. The effect may be short term or long term (it may even be the beginning of a new trend). Sometimes, the impact may not be as significant as we expect or it may be stronger than we thought. At times, what is happening in an economy would have little or no impact on the overall market biases – whether northward or southward. In some cases, the markets can skyrocket when the fundamentals are pessimistic. Yet, in other cases, the overall outlook on the markets can be in agreement with major fundamentals.

Generally, the global economies are interrelated. For instance, the events affecting the USD have impact on other countries, and the events affecting the EUR have impact on other currencies. Whenever a major instrument like gold or oil plummets, the trading world feels the impact, for example.

There are many good financial information websites that offer economic calendars free of charge. One of them is the popular Forexfactory.com (www.forexfactory.com/calendar.php). Here you can see the list of all fundamental figures expected for each trading day and the respective currencies they would affect. Each news items carries a certain colour:

Red: High impact is expected
Orange: Medium impact is expected
Yellow: Low impact is expected
White: News item which is non-economic

Normally, we are interested only in news items that come with the possibility of high impact (red). Many of these news items are available in most cases from Monday to Friday of each trading week. Personally, we are interested in the news items that come out every first Friday of the month, because on this particular day, we harness profits from the news items coming from the USA and Canada. The Trade Balance, Employment Change, Unemployment Rate figures etc, from other currencies like the Aussie and Cable are of major importance as well. However, in this chapter we focus on the ones coming from the USA and Canada.

We choose relevant pairs and crosses when looking forward to a particular news item. For example, when awaiting the Trade Balance figure from Canada, we consider every currency instrument that has the CAD as the base currency or the counter currency (USD/ CAD, CAD/JPY, EUR/CAD, AUD/CAD, CAD/CHF etc). Nevertheless, we do not want to choose any instrument with more than four pips, and therefore, we choose only the USD/CAD.

When awaiting the Trade Balance figure from the USA, we consider every currency instrument that has the USD as the base currency or the counter currency. Again, any of the major pairs is good provided the spread is four pips or less.

The Non-Farm Payroll

The NFP (Non-farm Payroll) fundamentals are important economic figures in the US. Their main purpose is to showcase the aggregate figure of paid employees in the United States (who are not working on farms, or for governments, charities and private households). The Non-farm Payroll figures trigger one of the greatest volatility arising from fundamentals in the markets. Because of this, a majority of currency strategists, fund managers and traders watch these figures and the kind of reactions they cause in the markets. Since many analysts and experts anticipate the figures and squawk about them, their impact is often spectacular even when figures come out as expected. The purpose of this piece is to show you one trading methodology that can be used to harness profits from NFP and other popular fundamental figures, especially the ones that are released on the first Friday of the month.

The first Friday of most months of the year is ideal for this strategy because of the perceptible quiet that usually happens in the market before the famous figures are released. The calm helps us make sure that any pre-news irrationality or volatility in the markets does not trigger any of the pending orders unnecessarily before the anticipated fundamental figures are released. As a result of this, we can set our pending orders about 15 minutes or ten minutes before the news is released. This kind of benefit is rarely enjoyed when trading the news on other days of the week. It is common for the

Non-farm Payroll to be released on the first Friday of every month at 8.30 am EST (1.30 pm GMT).

Recent News Trading Examples

You need a high-speed broadband Internet connection in order to use this method effectively; otherwise, don't try it. The charts that accompany this chapter were all taken on the same day. Naked charts are used for this trading method, for no indicators are needed. The red vertical line shows where a trade was entered. An open trade must be closed after three hours, even if the target has not been hit. In the examples, Buy Stops were the orders that were filled. In some order cases, it would be Sell-Stop orders. Spreads were not actually considered in the examples.

On Friday 5 April 2013, the trading world eagerly awaited a bunch of fundamental figures that would come out of the US and Canada. The expected time of release was 8.30 am EST (1.30 pm GMT). Below are the news items that were anticipated at that very time, plus their actual results:

CAD Employment Change: forecast = 6.8K, actual = −54.5K
CAD Trade Balance: forecast = 0.2B, actual = −1.0B
CAD Unemployment Rate: forecast = 7.1%, actual = 7.2%
USD Non-farm Employment Change: forecast = 198K, actual = 88K
USD Trade Balance: forecast = −44.8B, actual = −43.0B
USD Unemployment Rate: forecast = 7.7%, actual = 7.6%
Source: www.forexfactory.com/calendar.php

The figures had a negative impact on the CAD and a positive impact on the USD.

Trade A:

In Figure 1, it can be seen that the USD/CAD was in a quiet mode just before the news items were released. We set a Buy-Stop and a Sell-Stop order. The Sell-Stop Pending Order was immediately cancelled once the Buy-Stop order was triggered, and the trade resulted in a profit.

F1) Trade A: Buy Stop Triggered on the USD/CAD

The USD/CAD was in a quiet mode just before the news items were released.

Instrument: USD/CAD
Order: Buy-Stop
Entry date: 5 April 2013
Entry price: 1.0142
Stop loss: 1.0122
Take profit: 1.0202
Exit price: 1.0202
Profit/loss: 60 pips

Trade B:

The week in which Trade A was taken, the USD/JPY moved upwards by close to 500 pips. Two pending orders were set prior to this, but since the fundamental figures that were released on Friday were in favour of the extant bias, it was the Buy-Stop order that got filled. The Sell-Stop Pending Order was abruptly liquidated.

F2) Trade B: Buy Stop Activated on the USD/JPY

The week in which this trade was taken, the USD/JPY moved upwards by close to 500 pips.

Instrument: USD/JPY
Order: Buy-Stop
Entry date: 5 April 2013
Entry price: 95.95
Stop loss: 95.75
Take profit: 96.55
Exit price: 96.55
Profit/loss: 60 pips

Trade C:

In the early part of 2013, the Cable was in a significant downtrend. But at the time of making the trade below, the instrument was already rejecting any southward threats on it. A Buy-Stop and a Sell-Stop order were put in place, and the former was filled. The Sell-Stop Pending Order was quickly gotten rid of.

F3) Trade C: Buy Stop Was Filled on the GBP/USD

In the early part of the year 2013, the Cable was in a significant downtrend.

Instrument: GBP/USD
Order: Buy-Stop
Entry date: 5 April 2013
Entry price: 1.5150
Stop loss: 1.5130
Take profit: 1.5210
Exit price: 1.5210
Profit/loss: 60 pips

Conclusion

Top traders face uncertainties and unpredictability in the markets with confidence. They even maintain their sanity and emotional stability in the face of challenges in the markets. When this trading method is used properly, even a budding speculator can use it profitably. A gaunt hound can hunt down a squirrel. If you are already making profits from news trading, you have come a long way, but you still have many more profits to make in future. Success is possible.

Strategy Snapshot	
Strategy Name:	News Trading
Strategy Type:	Forex News Trading
Suitability:	Good for part-time and full-time traders
Time Horizon:	15-minute chart
Instruments Filter:	Do not trade on any pair or cross whose spread is greater than 4 pips
Setups:	Following the perceptible calm in the markets just before the news items get released, set a Buy-Stop pending order 20 pips away from the current price on your chosen instrument, and a Sell-Stop pending order 20 pips away from the current price on the chosen instrument
Stop Loss:	20 pips away from each pending order entry price
Take Profit:	60 pips away from each pending order entry price
Risk to Reward Ratio:	1:3
Position Sizing:	0.1 lots for each $1000 (and thus making it 1.0 lots for $10,000)
Maximum Trade Duration:	3 hours; quickly cancel one pending order once the other has been triggered

Scalping With Precision

High Probability Scalping
in Asian Sessions

Scalping the Forex markets on a short term basis can be highly profitable for disciplined scalpers. This is a trading style that makes you go for a few pips (or a little more) per trade. In most cases, orders are opened and closed in a matter of seconds or minutes. Scalping might be one of the best trading styles, if you do it flawlessly and control your emotions strictly. This chapter explains one way of scalping effectively.

Scalping The Markets Without Hesitation

Adeptness alone is not enough to make you an effective scalper. The essential thing is for you to execute orders with no hesitation. When prices are noisy, counter-trend moves are not overreacted to since they are viewed as something that must happen. Traders go long in an oversold market, expecting that the coming market journey will be favourable to them. Whereas in a downward market, the waves reveal some inexperienced surfers and the results are not good. The truth is this: The more assurance you need before you open positions, the less profitable the positions will be. This scalping strategy deals with the unpredictability of the markets in some form, after which you will be able to deal with the unpredictability with calm. You will no longer bother that your trades should not include any negativity, as that mindset can lead to self-sabotage. In this regard it is essential for some scalpers – those who do not yet think that trading should not be 100 per cent accurate.

When a runaway price is spotted, the order often goes positive immediately. Nonetheless, the price might retrace sharply, and it may cause your order to metamorphose from plus into minus, prior to metamorphosing to plus again, during another market retracement in your favour. When a trader does not have an open position, he/she may be looking for new trading opportunities, or merely whiling away the time waiting for the next favourite setups. The next setups can be helpful. To some extent, effective scalpers go short or long as early as it is sensible to do so, and close the order even as the price continues to tank further or rally. Yes, closing an order too early is still better than smoothing it too late. The outcome is that when scalpers scalp the markets with effectiveness and bravery, their account balance increases. Therefore when a scalper opens a trade and scalps with a signal, this requires a wise stop-loss, otherwise she/he will be affected by a premature exit and the tight stop would be unnecessarily hit.

Approaching the Markets With a Strategy

In most cases, markets do not travel in straight lines but oscillate within some trendlines. These territories could signify equilibrium zones, as they underpin the market unpredictability. A trading instrument will not go straight but instead gets pushed around accumulation and distribution zones. Whenever a market bias is terminated, for instance, when institutional traders smooth their positions and stay out of trading, serious equilibrium propensity develops. Trading in an equilibrium zone sometimes needs tried and tested speculation tools. If you prefer to be an intraday trader, you will encounter equilibrium zones most of the day, occasionally in the trading week, or in few months.

This trading system is ideal for the Asian Session, but is not compulsory for it. The currency markets are generally quiet and ideal for scalping during the Asian (Tokyo) Session, since prices tend to be more orderly and easily predictable on a near term basis. Scalping works better when the markets are in equilibrium zones and moving sideways, hence the reason we choose the trading period recommended in this chapter.

This is a period in which this strategy can better be traded effectively (see Strategy Snapshot). During summer, the Asian Session generally opens at 11.00 pm GMT (7.00 pm EST), and during winter, the Asian Session generally opens at 11.00 pm GMT (6.00 pm EST). However, the time zone in your country might be different. Entry condition must be valid on the two time frames. It helps to put your stop around a good demand zone (if you go long), or around a good supply zone (if you go short) since this would safeguard your trading in the short term. Prices would find it difficult to slash through these levels, except there is going to be a perpetually serious counter-trend reversal. You need to focus on the job at hand, do not ruin your trading day with side attractions and distractions. In a nutshell, nonetheless the chances of negativity and profitability are extant. That is why too high position sizing is not recommended. And it is not recommended that the maximum trading duration be exceeded, because if huge losses are incurred, they cannot be quickly replaced by small returns.

The Setup

The mixing of the simple indicators used here enables triggers for opening and smoothing orders. You buy when the SMA 50 crosses its SMA 90 counterpart to the upside and the RSI 14 is above the level 50, but not in the overbought region (the level at 70). You sell when the SMA 50 crosses the SMA 90 counterpart to the downside and the RSI 14 is below the level 50, but not in the oversold region (the level at 30). The entry criteria must be met on both the 1-minute and the 15-minute time frame. The short term trend is confirmed on the 15-minute chart while the signal is taken on the 1-minute chart. Although this is not used in trading examples in this chapter, you could add a filter in the equilibrium market, for instance, Bollinger Bands (default parameters). If the price is already pushing up the upper bands, you might not open a long order, and if the price is testing the lower bands constantly, you may not open a short order.

Trading Examples

In the trading examples below, 1-minute and 15-minute charts are juxtaposed for clarity. Spreads were not considered in the examples. In each figure, on the 1-minute chart, the vertical red line on the left shows where a trade was entered and the vertical red line on the right shows where it was exited. The blue indicator stands for the SMA 50 and the red indicator stands for the SMA 90. Likewise in each figure, on the 15-minute chart, a vertical red line shows where a scalping trade was taken in comparison to its 1-minute chart counterpart.

Example 1:

On 23 July 2012, the 15-minute chart indicated a downtrend as the 1-minute chart gave a short signal on the GBP/USD. At the time this signal was taken, the RSI 14 on the 1-minute chart was below the level 50, but not in the oversold region.

F1) A Short Signal Confirmation on the GBP/USD

The 15-minute chart (on the right) indicated a short term bear market as the 1-minute chart gave a short signal on the GBP/USD.

Instrument: GBP/USD
Order: Sell
Entry date: 23 July 2012
Entry price: 1.5555
Stop-loss: 1.5655
Take profit: 1.5545
Exit price: 1.5545
Profit/loss: 10 pips

Example 2:

In this trading example, there was a bearish signal confirmation on both the 1-minute and the 15-minute charts on 24 July 2012. A short-selling scalping order was taken and it hit the target soon after. Please note the position of the RSI 14 when the trade was taken.

F2) A Short Signal Confirmation on the EUR/USD

On the EUR/USD, there was a short term short signal on 24 July 2012.

Instrument: EUR/USD
Order: Sell
Entry date: 24 July 2012
Entry price: 1.2080
Stop-loss: 1.2180
Take profit: 1.2070
Exit price: 1.2070
Profit/loss: 10 pips

Example 3:

On the EUR/USD, there was a short term buy signal on 25 July 2012. This signal was confirmed on the 15-minute chart before the one on the 1-minute chart was taken. The scalping trade was successful.

F3) A Long Signal Confirmation on the EUR/USD

On the EUR/USD, there was a short term buy signal on 25 July 2012. this signal was confirmed on the 15-minute chart (on the right) before the one on the 1-minute chart was taken.

Instrument: EUR/USD
Order: Buy
Entry date: 25 July 2012
Entry price: 1.2122
Stop-loss: 1.2022
Take profit: 1.2132
Exit price: 1.2132
Profit/loss: 10 pips

Conclusion

Safeguarding your portfolio while remaining stolidly faithful to this scalping system may enhance our courage and foster more judicious use of our portfolios. We have to bear in mind that the end result of each order will be governed by chance, yet orders in the long run will possibly augment the value of our portfolios. Dr. Janice Dorn advises that we ought to treat each trade as a possible winner or a possible loser. There is absolutely no such thing as a "sure thing" in trading. Trading is a game of probabilities, and the goal is to make more than we lose. If we are in a strait jacket of perfectionism where everything has to work all the time, and we have to get just the bottom or just the top, and we cannot tolerate even one downtick, let alone a drawdown, then we are not suited to be traders. We strive for moderation and balance and eschew perfectionism, as it is one of our greatest enemies.

Strategy Snapshot	
Strategy Name:	Asian Session Scalper
Time Horizon:	1-minute and 15-minute charts
Trading Period:	It is ideal to trade from 11.00 pm GMT to 12.30 am GMT (you may mind the EST equivalent of this time period)
Indicator 1:	SMA period 50
Indicator 2:	SMA period 90
Indicator 3:	RSI 14, levels 30, 50 and 70
Currency Pairs:	EUR/USD and GBP/USD
Setup:	Buy when the SMA 50 crosses the SMA 90 counterpart to the upside and the RSI 14 is above the level 50, but not in the overbought region (the level at 70). Sell when the SMA 50 crosses the SMA 90 counterpart to the downside and the RSI is below the level 50, but not in the oversold region (the level at 30)
Entry Condition:	The entry criteria must be met on both the 1-minute and the 15-minute time frame. The short term trend is confirmed on the 15-minute chart while the signal is taken on 1-minute chart.
Stop:	100 pips from the entry price
Target:	5-10 pips
Trade Duration:	1.5 hours maximum

Exit Rule:	Close an open position after the maximum trade duration has expired
Alternative Exit Rule:	Close an order quickly if there is a fast reversal against you
Money Management:	Do not use more than 1 lot for each $10,000
Number of Orders per Day:	You may not take more than two trades per night (or a maximum of four trades if the market conditions are favourable). Generally, you are not expected to close more than two losses per night
Broker Preference:	Choose only brokers that support scalping. For example, some brokers do not require you to target less than 25 pips per trade

A Simple Position
Trading Strategy

Going After the Greatest Profit Potential

In stock and commodity markets, it is common for speculators and investors to hold positions for months, years, and even decades. This is also possible in Forex. Many Forex traders tend to talk only about intraday and swing trading approaches. So this is the reason why certain traders think position trading is not viable in Forex. It is viable. Position trading in Forex is a trading style in which you run a position for months or years before you exit it. Normally, a negative position is never to be run for as long as possible – only a positive position should be treated as such. Here is a helpful position trading method.

Exemplary Position Traders

There are many great position traders on this planet. Some are famous and some are not, but each one of them is successful in their own world. In one of his past newsletters from Tradingeducators.com, veteran trader Joe Ross recollected the greatest position trading he had personally seen. The position was managed by a long term speculator, and it lasted for about ten years (1991 to 2000). The speculator opened the position on the S&P 500 in early December, 1991, and smoothed it in 2000. This man speculated on a higher time frame, applying a trailing stop. The trailing stop was employed when it was felt that a good gain had been made. Moving from the daily chart to the weekly chart, the speculator continued to manage the position. Ultimately, the position ended up making a $16,000,000 gain.

Another famous position trader/investor was Philip A. Fisher (8 September 1907 to 11 March 2004). This shy soul, who authored "Common Stocks and Uncommon Profits," gained many followers, including Warren Buffett himself. Philip was disciplined enough to hold his trades for very long periods of time. He invested in good companies with highly encouraging facts and figures, and he attained enviable goals in the markets (excellent profits). He went long on Motorola in 1955 and held onto that position until he died at the age of 96.

Position Trading in Forex

As a Forex trader, if you had shorted the GBP/CHF in July 2007 and held it till now, you would have gained far more than 10,000 pips on that single trade. If you had gone long on the EUR/USD at the beginning of the year 2001 and held it until the beginning of the year 2007, you could have gained more than 7,300 pips on that position alone. If you had sold the EUR/AUD from the beginning of 2009 and held onto it till now, you could have gained more than 7,000 pips as profits on the position. If EUR/NZD had been shorted (at the same time the EUR/AUD was sold) and held till now, you would have gained far more than 9,000 pips on that. There are far bigger profits to be made by riding the primary trends for as long as they last, but, unfortunately, most of us do not have the patience and discipline to do this.

Patience is an absolute must and a requisite for this trading method. It is a quality that is needed to stick to the entry rule, to apply trading management operations to an open position, to run a position for as long as it is valid, and to exit, when there is a clear signal to do so. When a currency instrument enters a protracted equilibrium phase, it does not mean that it cannot eventually go in the forecasted direction, no matter how protracted the equilibrium phase may be. One just needs to stick to the entry and exit rules. Needless to say, this trading method doesn't make sense for those who lack incessant patience while trading.

The position trading method that is featured in this chapter makes use of the Stochastic Oscillator (the default parameters) on the weekly chart. The only difference is that the indicator is set to have three levels: levels 80, 50 and 20. On a specified instrument, we assume a long position after the Stochastic Oscillator has come out of the oversold territory and crossed the level 50 to the upside. Likewise, we assume a short position after the Stochastic Oscillator has come out of overbought territory and crossed level 50 to the downside. It should be noted that the Stochastic Oscillator is overbought when it is above level 80 and oversold when it is below level 20. For further details of the strategy, please look at the Strategy Snapshot at the end of the chapter.

Position Trading Examples

It should be pointed that only strongly trending pairs and crosses are ideal for this strategy, and therefore, spreads are irrelevant (no matter how high they may be), because a position is run for as long as possible and gains are maximised. Some of the strongly trending pairs and crosses are GBP/USD, GBP/CAD, GBP/CHF, GBP/AUD, GBP/NZD, EUR/AUD, EUR/NZD, EUR/CAD, AUD/USD, NZD/USD etc. The list also includes all JPY pairs.

The vertical red line on the left shows where a position was opened, and the vertical red line on right shows where it was exited. The initial stop, break-even stop, and trailing stop are large enough to allow optimal room for normal and crazy volatility/fluctuations, so that premature exits can be prevented.

Example 1:

Look at Figure 1. In 2008, on the GBP/JPY, the Stochastic was in a constant overbought territory for about 14 weeks. Soon, the cross began to weaken, and finally there was a clean 'sell' signal in the market. This signal was capitalised on; it was smoothed 27 weeks later in a plus zone. The exit signal was generated before the position was smoothed, and as a result, some part of the profit was sacrificed, otherwise the percentage profit would have been more than 45 per cent. Even if there was an unusual circumstance in the market which went against the position trader, about 50 per cent of the profit had already been safeguarded by the trailing stop.

F1) Shorting the Weak GBP/JPY

In 2008, on the GBP/JPY, the Stochastic was in constantly overbought territory for about 14 weeks.

Instrument: GBP/JPY
Order: Sell
Entry date: August 2008
Entry price: 210.50
Stop-loss: 215.50
Trailing stop: 170.50
Take profit: 121.50
Exit date: February 2009

Trade duration: 27 weeks
Profit/loss: 8100+ pips
Percentage gain: 40%+

Example 2:

Figure 2 shows an extant long position. This position, which is already in a plus zone, will be run for as long as the Stochastic stays above level 50. In early April 2013, on the GBP/ AUD chart, the Stochastic rose from its oversold territory and crossed level 50 to the upside. No sooner had this happened than a long position was opened. The break-even stop and the trailing stop have been put in place. The Stochastic is currently in overbought territory, since the market is in a very strong northward bias. At the time of writing this chapter, the GBP/AUD was trading at 1.6478. You should also note that there are past profitable signals on the chart.

F2) An Extant Long Position on the GBP/AUD

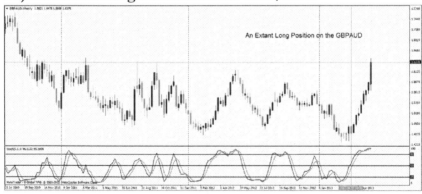

An extant long position is already in a plus zone, and will be run for as long as the Stochastic stays above the level 50.

Instrument: GBP/AUD
Order: Buy
Entry date: April 2013
Entry price: 1.4645
Stop-loss: 1.4145
Trailing stop: 1.5545
Take profit: N/A
Exit date: N/A
Trade duration: 8 weeks so far
Profit/loss: 1,800+ pips
Percentage gain: 9%+

Example 3:

In Figure 3, a losing position is depicted. The position first went in the expected direction by a few hundred pips before the price dropped (owing to some volatile bearish pressure in the market). Since the recommended risk control and position sizing rules were applied, the negativity was put under control and it had no effect on the account. This was possible because the stop was set to break-even as soon as the initial gain got up to 200 pips. Even if the stop was hit, it would still have no significant effect on the portfolio. Any recent or subsequent positive position that was/is allowed to run would more than compensate for this.

F3) A Potential Loss Was averted in EUR/CAD

The position first went in the expected direction by a few hundreds of pips before the price dropped (owing to some volatile bearish pressure in the market).

Instrument: EUR/CAD
Order: Sell
Entry date: October 2008
Entry price: 1.6010
Stop-loss: 1.5510
Break-even stop: 1.6010
Exit price: 1.6010
Exit date: October 2008
Trade duration: 3 weeks
Profit/loss: 0 pips
Percentage gain: 0%

Conclusion

Do not hesitate, when you are provided with a clear signal. You should not smooth your position too soon; run your profit. You should exit only when you get a clean exit signal on the weekly chart.

1. Do not open more than four positions at once.

2. Do not exceed the recommended position sizing and stop-loss, especially when you are trying to recoup previously sustained negativity.

3. Even when a position is exited with a degree of negativity, it does not mean that it cannot be recovered in the future. It is only a matter of time.

The things you worry about most usually never happen. The vicissitudes of position trading could be encountered triumphantly – just as it is true of other trading styles. There might be challenges in the first few months or years, however, being in the trading profession has brought us joy and blessings beyond all measure.

Strategy Snapshot	
Strategy Name:	Stochastic Position Trading Strategy
Strategy Type:	Position Trading
Suitability:	Position and part-time traders
Time Horizon:	Weekly charts
Indicator:	Stochastic Oscillator (with default parameters)
Long Entry Rule:	When the Stochastic comes out of the oversold territory and crosses the level 50 to the upside, go long immediately
Short Entry Rule:	When the Stochastic comes down from the overbought territory and crosses the level 50 to the downside, go short immediately
Initial Stop:	500 pips from the entry price
Trade Management:	Move your stop to break-even once you have gained up to 200 pips per position. From 400-pip profit upwards, apply 50% trailing stop for your gains
Position Sizing:	0.01 lots for each $2000
Risk per Trade:	2.5%
Exit:	For a long position, exit when the Stochastic crosses the level 50 to the downside. For a short position, exit when the Stochastic crosses the level 50 to the upside; otherwise, a position is exited when the stop or the trailing stop is hit
Maximum Number of Open Trades:	4
Hit Rate:	Less than 30%

Speculating on Long-term Pullbacks

Good Bargains on higher Timeframes

Forex trading is becoming more and more appealing to those who used to specialize in stocks, futures, spread betting and other types of financial markets. Swing and position trading approaches in the currency markets are often preferred by seasoned traders. Competitive spreads and ever present trending instruments are really tempting! One such approach that can be used by both beginner and seasoned traders is explained here. It is about sustained pullbacks in the markets. Trading pullbacks on higher timeframes can be highly rewarding as well as stress-free, provided one employs a trading approach that works and applies safety measures that enable one to be indifferent to an individual position.

Promising Long-term Pullbacks

On a higher timeframe like a weekly chart, a pullback may be significant enough to threaten an extant primary trend. It may even violate it and end up overriding the trend. Whether a pullback is simply a medium–term threat to the dominant bias or the beginning of a new dominant bias, it is possible to make gains from it. It is common for a medium-term pullback to move by hundreds of pips before the price respects a dominant bias; likewise it is possible for the pullback to move by several hundred pips before it ends up overriding the dominant bias. How one can take advantage of these kinds of price actions is detailed below.

The Indicators for the Trading Method

As it is mentioned above, our purpose is to trade a significant sale in the context of an uptrend or a significant rally in a context of a downtrend, whether or not the sale or the rally ends up rendering the extant dominant bias invalid. Really it is suicidal to trade every technical northward bounce in a downtrend or every technical southward correction in an uptrend. This is why this trading method is designed in a way that allows you to trade a pullback that has been judged as having the potential to move determinedly in the forecasted direction.

The indicators used are Bollinger Bands period 20 (having the Upper Line, the Lower Line and the Middle Line), the Commodity Channel Index period 14 (having the levels 100, 50 and –100), and the Simple Moving Average Period 200.

For us to buy long, we would need to make sure that the downtrend has been in place for a long period of time, making lower lows and lower highs. In this kind of scenario, we would see that the price has been testing and breaching the Lower Line of the BB as the CCI ventures constantly into the oversold territory. At that period, the SMA 200 would be trending downwards and the price would be below it. With this scenario, there is a Bearish Confirmation Pattern on the chart. When would we then buy long? Usually the scenario described here is not a trading signal at all. It simply alerts us to the possibility of the price pulling back significantly very soon.

Once the BB crosses the Middle Band to the upside, and the CCI leaves its area below the level 50 (crossing the level to the upside), and the price has crossed the SMA 200 to the upside, then a bullish signal is in place. At this time, one would see that the SMA 200 which was formerly acting as a barrier to the bulls' interests is now acting as a support to them.

The Lot Sizes

It is imperative that we stick to the recommended lot sizes for this method. We should also make sure that a negative position does not run beyond our initial stop.

Experts agree among themselves that very high lot sizes and running of negative orders will never be favourable to any trader in the long run. Since the currency pair or cross that you trade does not know whether you are long or short, just make sure you do not shoot yourself in the foot yourself by running your order against the reality on the chart. The lot sizes are small, bringing seemingly small profits, but smaller losses as well. What are seen as seemingly small profits would translate into something substantial over time. To be slow and sure is better than to be fast and foolish.

The trading method is very good for those who like to look at the big picture and capitalize on its tricky nuances. It is also good for those who are very busy with other activities and would like to play the markets strictly on a part-time basis, while they spend less than one hour per week looking for signals and managing existing trades. On the charts, the BB is given magenta colour, the CCI is given blue colour (its levels are dim grey), and the SMA 200 is given red colour. All the entry conditions must be satisfied before a position is taken. There is a vertical red line where a trade is taken and a vertical red line where it is smoothed. Spreads were not considered in the trades shown here. Actually, spreads do not matter much where a position is taken with hundreds of pips in the stop area and several hundreds of pips in the target area.

Trade A

Please see Figure 1. In May 2012, the CADJPY tested the Lower Band of the BB and it would be seen that the CCI also went into the oversold territory at that period. The SMA 200 is trending lower. This shows that the dominant bias is bearish in spite of the palpable turbulence that has taken place before the signal is generated. We waited for a rally, which occurred in July/August as the CCI crossed the level 50 to the upside and the price crossed the Middle Band of the BB to the upside. This situation made us anticipate a long position with great eagerness: as soon as the price crossed the SMA 200 to the upside and closed above it, a long position was opened which ended up reaching its target in about 9 weeks.

F1) A Long Position on the CADJPY

We took a long position on the CADJPY.

Instrument: CADJPY
Order: Buy
Entry date: 25 November 2012
Entry price: 83.00
Stop loss: 80.00
Trailing stop: 87.50
Take profit: 92.00
Status: Closed

Profit/loss: 900 pips

Percentage gain: 4.5%

Trade B

Towards the end of the year 2012 and the beginning of the year 2013, the BB had been narrow (a squeeze), while the price tested the Upper Level a few times. During this period, the CCI was twice in the overbought territory but could not go below the level 50, following the first foray into the overbought territory. The SMA was sloping upwards in spite of the volatility in the market; which means that the bulls held sway. This made us get ready for a possible confirmation of a bearish signal. In May 2013, the confirmation was seen when the price crossed the SMA to the downside and closed below it. In the following week, a short position was assumed, and the take profit was reached before the market experienced another significant correction. This is illustrated in Figure 2.

F2) A Short Position on the AUDUSD

Around the beginning of the year 2013, the BB had been narrow (a squeeze), while the price tested the Upper Level a few times.

Instrument: AUDUSD
Order: Sell
Entry date: 19 May 2013
Entry price: 0.9835
Stop loss: 1.0135
Trailing stop: 0.9385
Take profit: 0.8935
Status: Closed
Profit/loss: 900 pips
Percentage gain: 4.5%

Heroes Do Not Panic

In the word of Rick Wright, everything has its positives and negatives. This is true of any trading method under heaven, including the one being discussed here. A trading approach goes into a crisis when a loss is made or things do not go according to the speculator's expectation. Crises are necessary to test what you believe. The vicissitudes of trading will test your commitment to trading success. An undisciplined trader may abandon a good trading method after a grave negativity which comes as a result of lack of discipline. Whether the method is abandoned or not, the damage has already been done to the undisciplined trader. The knife cuts one's finger, and one throws it away in anger. The knife has already accomplished its mission.

Trade C

Figure 3 shows us a good lesson. In this instance, a bearish signal was generated on the GBPUSD on May 20, 2012; thus we sold short according to the criteria of the method. Within two weeks, we gained more than 500 pips. We had already been applying the recommended 50% trailing stop (once the profit reached up to 300 pips). Unfortunately, during the third week, there was a massive northward push by the bulls – something that rendered our bearish outlook invalid. The trailing stop prevented the trade from going towards negativity: the trade was closed at 250 pips. Heroes do not panic.

F3) Abortive but Successful Signals

There is a lesson to be learned from two signals on this chart. (1) A trade that doesn't reach its target could still be closed with a profit. (2) Even when a stop is hit, subsequent signals may recoup the negligible negativity.

Instrument: AUDUSD
Order: Sell
Entry date: 20 May 2012
Entry price: 1.5830
Stop loss: 1.6130
Trailing stop: 1.5580
Take profit: 1.4930
Status: Closed
Profit/loss: 250 pips
Percentage gain: 1.25%

Yes, heroes do not panic! The worst thing that could have happened to us here was to lose 1.5% of the total portfolio, which we would be indifferent to, because it would be insignificant and because subsequent positions based on valid setups would probably recover the negligible negativity. On 27 January 2013 (in the same Figure 3), another bearish signal on the GBPUSD would also have been taken according to our criteria. The position would have been opened at the formation of the candle that shows on top of the small Arrow Up on the chart. This signal was favourable to us, almost reaching our target before the price shot upwards. Even if our target was not reached, our 50% trailing stop rule would have helped us take about 450 pips as gain. This would translate into 2.25% gain. Let us bear this lesson in mind.

Conclusion

Possibly the most important aspect of speculation is one's faithfulness to one's trading rules and perseverance at the time one is experiencing a transitory drawdown. When you focus on what you didn't get, it's too easy to forget all of what you did get. This trading methodology is designed to lose as little as possible while it gains as much as possible. What does that mean? It means that occasional negativity would usually be negligible and winnings would be moderately substantial. You may thus want to practice with this trading method for about six months, so that you can personally experience its potential yourself; after which you may go live. Everybody who has achieved extraordinary goals in any field of human endeavour has constantly practiced for that.

Strategy Snapshot	
Strategy Name:	Pullback Signaller
Strategy Type:	Position trading
Suitability:	Good for part-time traders
Time Horizon:	Weekly charts
Indicator 1:	Bollinger Bands (BB) period 20
Indicator 2:	Commodity Channels Index (CCI) period 14
Indicator 3:	Simple Moving Average (SMA) period 200

Long Entry:	In an oversold downtrend, buy long when the BB has crossed the Middle Line to the upside, the CCI has moved upwards from its oversold territory (crossing the level 50 to the upside), and the SMA 200 is below the price which has crossed it and closed above it
Short Entry:	In an overbought uptrend, sell short when the BB has crossed the Middle Line to the downside, the CCI has moved downwards from its overbought territory (crossing the level 50 to the downside), and the SMA 200 is above the price which has just crossed it and closed below it
Lot Sizes:	Use 0.01 lots for each $1000 (and thus making it 0.1 lots for $10000); or 0.1 lots for each 20000 cents in a cent account (making it 1.0 lots for each 100000 cents)
Stop:	300 pips
Target:	900 pips
Risk per Trade:	1.5%
Potential Reward per Trade:	4.5%
Breakeven Stop:	Move your stop to breakeven after you have gained at least 100 pips
Trailing Stop:	Apply a 50% trailing stop after you have gained up to 300 pips
Limitation:	Do not hold more than 4 open positions at a time
Maximum Trade Duration:	3 months. An open position is smoothed after 3 months, whether it is positive or negative

About the Author

Azeez Mustapha is a trading professional, funds manager, an InstaForex official analyst, a blogger at ADVFN.com, and a freelance author for trading magazines. He works as a trading signals provider at various websites and his numerous articles are posted on many websites such as www.ituglobalforex.blogspot.com.

Contact: azeez.mustapha@analytics.instaforex.com.

This is Azeez's third book for ADVFN Books. Turn over for details of his first two.

Also by Azeez Mustapha

Learn From
the Generals
of the Market

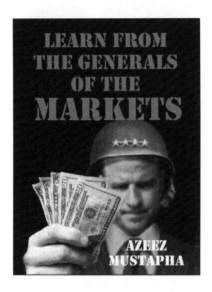

If you want to win on the trading battlefield, you need the right ammunition.

Trading is like any other profession: to succeed, you need to arm yourself with the necessary skills. Enter the arena without knowing what you are doing, and you are sure to lose your money.

You need help from the experts.

Learn From the Generals of the Markets profiles twenty renowned super traders from around the world, great traders who know what it takes to be successful in the markets. The book gives an overview of their careers and explains what lessons can be drawn from their success, so you can apply their methods and techniques to your own trading. It will help you gain the expertise you need to improve your prospects.

This essential guide should be part of every trader's armament.

Available in paperback and for the Kindle from Amazon.

What Super Traders Don't Want You to Know

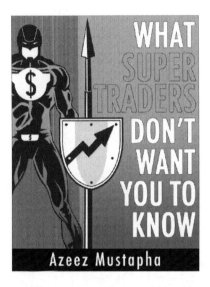

If you want to succeed as a trader, you need to learn the necessary skills.

Risk your money on the markets without knowing what you are doing, and you could lose it all. Just like any other profession, to be a trader requires you to learn from the experts.

What Super Traders Don't Want You To Know profiles twenty-two renowned super traders from around the world, great traders who know what it takes to be successful in the markets. In this follow up to his previous book *Learn From the Generals of the Markets*, Azeez Mustapha gives an overview of their careers and explains what lessons can be drawn from their success.

You can apply their methods and techniques to your own trading, and gain the expertise you need to improve your prospects.

This essential guide could start you on the path to becoming a super trader.

Available in paperback and for the Kindle from Amazon.

More Books from ADVFN

101 Charts for Trading Success

by Zak Mir

Using insider knowledge to reveal the tricks of the trade, Zak Mir's *101 Charts for Trading Success* explains the most complex set ups in the stock market.

Providing a clear way of predicting price action, charting is a way of making money by delivering high probability percentage trades, whilst removing the need to trawl through company accounts and financial ratios.

Illustrated with easy to understand charts this is the accessible, essential guide on how to read, understand and use charts, to buy and sell stocks. *101 Charts* is a must for all future investment millionaires.

Available in paperback and for the Kindle from Amazon.

The Great Oil Price Fixes and How to Trade Them

by Simon Watkins

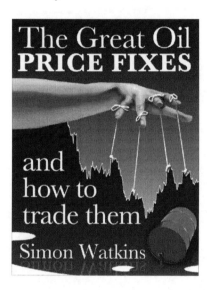

The oil market has been manipulated to an extremely high degree for decades, both overtly and covertly, and given its enduring geopolitical importance that is likely to continue.

Traders need to understand the essential dynamics that drive the global oil market, offering as it does unparalleled opportunities to make returns over and above those of other markets. The oil market is also an essential part of trading FX, equities, bonds and other commodities.

Simon Watkins' book The Great Oil Price Fixes And How To Trade Them offers you the knowledge you need. It covers the history of the market, gives you an understanding of the players in the oil game, and provides a solid grounding in the market-specific trading nuances required in this particular field.

The essential elements of the general trading methodology, strategies and tactics that underpin top professional traders are covered with reference to how they can be used to trade in the oil market.

Available in paperback and for the Kindle from Amazon.

The Game in Wall Street

by Hoyle and Clem Chambers

As the new century dawned, Wall Street was a game and the stock market was fixed. Ordinary investors were fleeced by big institutions that manipulated the markets to their own advantage and they had no comeback.

The Game in Wall Street shows the ways that the titans of rampant capitalism operated to make money from any source they could control. Their accumulated funds gave the titans enormous power over the market and allowed them to ensure they won the game.

Traders joining the game without knowing the rules are on a road to ruin. It's like gambling without knowing the rules and with no idea of the odds.

The Game in Wall Street sets out in detail exactly how this market manipulation works and shows how to ride the price movements and make a profit.

And guess what? The rules of the game haven't changed since the book was first published in 1898. You can apply the same strategies in your own investing and avoid losing your shirt by gambling against the professionals.

Illustrated with the very first stock charts ever published, the book contains a new preface and a conclusion by stock market guru Clem Chambers which put the text in the context of how Wall Street operates today.

Available in paperback and for the Kindle from Amazon.

For more information on these books and out other titles, go to the ADVFN Books website at www.advfnbooks.com.

ADVFN BOOKS